Penguin Education

Penguin Papers in Education

D0562123

Young Teachers and Reluctant Learners
Charles Hannam, Pat Smyth and Norman Stephenson

Young Teachers and Reluctant Learners

An account of the Hillview project,
an experiment in teacher education, and a discussion
of its educational implications

Charles Hannam, Pat Smyth
and Norman Stephenson

Penguin Books

Penguin Books Ltd, Harmondsworth,
Middlesex, England
Penguin Books Inc., 7110 Ambassador Road,
Baltimore, Md 21207, USA
Penguin Books Australia Ltd,
Ringwood, Victoria, Australia

First published 1971
Reprinted 1972
Copyright © Charles Hannam, Pat Smyth
and Norman Stephenson, 1971

Made and printed in Great Britain by
Hazell Watson & Viney Ltd, Aylesbury, Bucks
Set in Linotype Times

Contents

Preface

Young Teachers and Reluctant Learners is an account of a scheme, which we here call the Hillview project, designed to help young teachers in training to get to know and begin to understand the lives and values of working-class children. The children were aged fifteen and were for the most part on the verge of leaving school. The project involves the student teachers in informal relationships and does not require that they should teach the children in any conventional sense. Yet because of the depth and duration of the relationships formed it seems to us to throw some light on the sources of the difficulty that all teachers have with such children. It perhaps offers too some insight into the clash of values between teachers and so-called reluctant learners, and into their virtual inability to communicate with one another. The structure of authority and the institutional constraints of secondary schools do little to ease a difficult situation. This account of the project may contribute also to the current discussion of the reform of teacher training, often criticized for failing to prepare teachers adequately to provide an education for *all* children of secondary-school age.

For obvious reasons we have had to preserve the anonymity of the schools, teachers, students and children who have made our work possible and to whom we are very grateful. We have changed the names of all persons and places, but nothing else. We regret very much that we cannot acknowledge by name the students who have been involved, but we hope that they will accept this expression of our indebtedness. Much of our evidence derives from their journals and contributions in discussion, though the interpretations are our responsibility.

We have been encouraged in this work by colleagues and would particularly like to thank Ann Low-Beer, Colin Bayne-Jardine, Nancy Martin and Pam Hannam, who have read and commented helpfully on parts of the manuscript. Finally we are grateful to the Bristol University School of Education, which has made a small grant of money to pay for the running costs of the project.

Chapter 1
The Problem

Secondary education for all is widely accepted in principle, but is still far from being achieved in practice. It is true that all children now stay on at school at least until they are fifteen years old, and in 1972–3 the school-leaving age will be raised a further year. New schools are being built, existing ones are being reorganized on comprehensive lines, and there is a growing investment in curriculum research and development. Despite all this, evidence continues to accumulate that many children gain little from what is offered to them. Moreover, teachers themselves are divided over the wisdom of extending the period of education for young adolescents, whose awkward behaviour and apparent reluctance to learn have always presented problems. Teacher-training institutions play their part in the effort to expand secondary education by producing more teachers, but there is a growing concern that their courses are not sufficiently geared to the reality of the school situation.

Our work in the postgraduate division of a school of education has raised the issues very sharply. Traditionally, university departments have prepared students to teach in grammar schools, and the course of training has been based on the assumption that they would for the most part teach children for whom secondary education was evidently meaningful. With the development of comprehensive schools the situation has changed radically. A large number of our students work in such schools during their training year, and a growing proportion take up permanent posts in them. Here they will meet children of all kinds, including the 'difficult' ones who rarely find their way into grammar schools. We realized that many of the students were finding their teaching-practice experience in comprehensive schools so frustrating that they seriously questioned the value of the whole course we provided for them. It seemed that the stress of the practical classroom situation

prevented them from making any effective use either of theoretical studies in education or of methodological work in the
teaching of their special subject. We shall in this book describe a
project which, among other aims, attempts to bring theory and
practice into a more satisfactory relationship. Before we do this
we want to analyse in more detail some of the difficulties which
stand in the way of effective teacher training.

The most familiar charge against all training institutions is
that the theoretical studies in education – philosophy, psycho-
logy, sociology and so on – are presented in too abstract a way
to be of value to the intending teacher. He seems to find it difficult to make the connection between these disciplines and his
urgent need to establish his competence in the classroom. Part
of the difficulty perhaps lies in the way these studies are presented. Traditionally, courses of lectures are provided on the
assumption that by this means students are exposed to those
disciplines which contribute to the study of education. There
are however certain features about the lecture as a method of
teaching that militate against effective learning. Too often it
serves primarily as a demonstration of the authority of the
lecturer as an expert in his field. The assumption is made that
the student has sufficient familiarity with the subject area to
provide a context for the ideas presented and the terminology
used. In fact it is only when the student is in a position to
know what he wants from a lecture that he is generally able to
profit from it, and this is rarely the case with those who are
beginning their professional training. Where the lecture
succeeds as a demonstration of authority the student is left in
a state of dependence, convinced only of his lack of expertise.
A few may be stimulated to discover more for themselves, but
it is our impression that many finish up doubting even the
validity of their own relevant experience. For instance, we find
that our students, after sixteen years of being educated, often
maintain they know nothing about education and can make no
valid contribution to any discussion of it. Although lectures of
this kind have long been under attack as an effective method
of teaching they continue to dominate courses in education, as

though they were emblematic of true learning. Like Tibetan prayer flags fluttering in the wind they follow their pre-ordained course, whether comprehended or not, as if their mere existence were evidence of academic worth. It is not that the lecture has no place in a teacher-training programme. Once a context has been established, the orderly presentation of issues and concepts may contribute usefully to learning and take its place alongside seminars and discussion groups.

The context we speak of is in part provided by the specific requirements of the practical school situation – certainly students often regard school practice as the most profitable part of their education course. Yet the usual arrangement of blocks of theory presented in relatively abstract terms inter-spersed with blocks of 'real' experience in schools has serious limitations. Such an arrangement tends to make students under-value the importance of theory, and see their prime task as establishing themselves as quickly as possible as competent practitioners. They feel under pressure to win the approval of teachers, heads and their supervising tutors, and are reluctant to conceive of themselves as learners in a developing situation. It is right that students should want to assure themselves that they are able to operate effectively in the teaching role, and any course concerned with initial teacher training must provide an extended period in schools so that this can happen. Yet it is by no means certain that the best way to prepare them for this is to plunge them directly into the complexity of class teaching. A gradual introduction is likely to be more effective – through work with small groups of children, through collaboration with one another on joint projects, supported all the time by discus-sion with tutors and with one another and by constructive analysis of the work that has been done. Moreover, such a variety of approach will broaden the student's concept of what teaching is about. It may help him to move away from the narrow model which he may be driven to follow by his anxiety to prove himself as a class teacher from the outset.

At present the student finds himself placed in a school where he is expected, and expects himself, to operate effectively with neither the experience nor the means to do so. The student in school is typically the 'marginal man': he has left the security of the training institution, but he has no clearly defined status in the organizational structure of the school. He feels that to the children he is *only* a student, to the staff an intruder in the staffroom who is, reluctantly or not, given classes to teach but who is not fully accepted as a colleague. In addition to this uncertainty about his role in the school, he has to cope with the anxieties arising from his continuing relationship with the college or education department. He will have a supervisor who will visit the school from time to time to give what help he can, but also to assess his competence. Too often these visits are felt to be threatening, since the supervisor coming in from outside cannot fully appreciate the complexity of the student's situation. Visits are usually too infrequent to offer anything like continuous support – yet if the supervisor *does* visit often the student may be overwhelmed by feelings of inadequacy.

The teacher in the school may have feelings of ambivalence towards these visits. He may well see the supervisor as a potential critic of his own work and be resentful of his apparent remoteness from the rigours of day-to-day class teaching. His doubts may be passed on to the student, contributing further to his sense of isolation. The student is in a difficult position: he has somehow to come to terms with the varying demands made upon him. It is not surprising that he is often tempted into manipulating one side against the other. To his supervisor he may represent the school as unhelpful and incompetent; to the school he may describe both supervisor and the training institution as out of touch and impractical. When the supervisor announces a visit the student may enlist the help of the staff to 'defeat' him. Everyone, including the children, may conspire to lay on a 'good lesson': one that satisfies what are believed to be the supervisor's requirements, and covers up any sign of conflict or difficulty. If this strategy is not possible and things do not go smoothly, the student may be tempted to win the supervisor's sympathy by gaining his agreement that the school is at fault or the children impossible. None of these manoeuvres enables any party to tackle realistically the actual problem: the need for a cooperative approach to the student-teacher's learning.

Part of the difficulty is that the proper relations between school and teacher-training institution have never been satisfactorily worked out. It is assumed by teacher trainers that the responsibility for students' learning in the practical situation is shared between them and the teachers. For the most part, in our experience, teachers see it rather differently. As members of the institution of the school they are forced to identify with its values, owing their first loyalty to fellow-teachers and the children and regarding the students as a burden placed on them by those whose paid function is precisely to shoulder it themselves. The more privileged position of those in teacher-training institutions, and their better pay and working conditions, do not make matters any easier. Because the boundaries of the differing roles of schoolteacher and teacher trainer have not been defined, the way is open to the 'school-practice game'. The teacher, having taken on the student, may see himself as his protector against the supervisor, covering up the real sources of the student's difficulties, becoming overprotective to the point of assuring the supervisor that things are much better when he is not there. A further development of this tactic is to avoid the supervisor altogether or to arrange meetings in such a way that no real discussion can take place. Alternatively, the teacher can take up a hostile stance to the student: he may avoid the supervisor until the last possible moment, and then reveal deficiencies and faults too late for anything constructive to be done. A related ploy is the school's demand that it should be sent 'good' students only, with often enough an implication that less immediately successful students must be a neglected product of the college or department of education.

The supervisor inevitably joins in with this game. A quick visit ensures that he avoids painful contacts with the staff of the school, the more time he spends with the student the less he is available for consultation with the teacher. As a result of this

he may be open to manipulation by the student into a negatively critical attitude to the school. Part of the problem of the
supervisor is that, as things are, he and the student are in schools
on sufferance, and he has to take care to preserve the goodwill
of the school. The game demands that supervisor and teacher
go through a ritual dance of polite but non-committal exchange
of views, apparently designed to avoid any genuine consultation. Yet it is quite clear that only through consultation at all
stages between teachers in schools and supervisors in colleges
and departments can school practice be made an effective part
of teacher training. The essential part that teachers play in the
process as an aspect of their professional status must be openly
recognized and rewarded.

Teachers, of course, do not operate as entirely free agents:
their freedom of action is limited by the nature of the institution they and the children work in. The structure of schools
is hierarchical: head teacher, deputy head, heads of houses,
heads of departments, assistant teachers and pupils. Decisions
concerning the running of the institution are made at the top
and filter down to the teacher in the classroom. Generally the
head is the sole point of contact between the institution and
the outside world. He operates on the boundary, insulating his
staff from interference, though at the same time asserting his
power by cutting them off from access to higher authority –
governors, education officers and the like. In some respects
schools are like prisons and hospitals: they are based on nine-
teenth-century models and as institutions have scarcely come to
terms with twentieth-century needs. They are basically authoritarian in structure, paternalistic in their attitude to the inmates,
and insulated from the world at large. Though schools are not
'total' institutions – both teachers and children spend a proportion of their time at home – attendance is compulsory, the staff
have complete control over children, both are expected to conform to a narrowly defined code of behaviour, and there are
sanctions on all to ensure compliance. All institutions of this
kind have not only a primary function – to restore patients to
health, to contain and reform criminals, to educate children –

but also secondary functions which can easily obscure the main task. Chief among these is simply the institution's determination to preserve its own orderly existence, a determination which can easily swamp the main task. So, in hospitals patients may be woken up to be given sleeping pills, in prisons the socially inadequate are deprived of all initiative, and in schools an insistence upon obedience and punctuality may take precedence over the development of independent thought. Where such a tendency is not recognized and checked, the institution can become autocratic in its mode of functioning.

Although not all secondary schools can fairly be described as autocratic, they have sufficient characteristics of total institutions to subject the teacher to considerable pressure. The structure of the school being generally authoritarian, the teacher has one of several responses open to him. He may identify with the system wholeheartedly, because he has the kind of personality which finds this mode of functioning acceptable; or, on a more conscious level, he may calculate that his submission to the system and his support of it will be rewarded by official approval and promotion. Teachers who respond like this will wish to avoid conflict with authority because of their dependence on it. They will tend to be unsympathetic to suggestions for change, whether they come from inside or outside the school. It may be that institutions such as schools attract people who wish for this kind of security. It is difficult to say how many teachers are of this kind, but certainly there is considerable resistance to change in secondary schools, even in such relatively minor matters as school uniform or the prefect system. Such teachers too may be less than welcoming to the interruptions which students, and the responsibility they bring with them, are bound to cause.

The second response to the situation may be somewhat more ambivalent. The teacher may not wholly accept the authoritarian structure but his relative powerlessness may cause him to withdraw from any responsibility for the running of the institution. He may feel that he is employed simply to teach his subject and willingly accept whatever those above decide should be done. This position can only be maintained by a denial of feeling and a loss of self-esteem. A more constructive response, though one essentially of the same kind, is when the teacher, feeling alienated from the school as an institution, becomes totally immersed in his relationship with the children. Undoubtedly teachers in this situation can encourage effective learning, but only at the cost of considerable conflict. Such a teacher's work with children is limited by the lack of support from the school as a whole. He will find himself enforcing rules which he has taken no part in drawing up, and he may be tempted to over-identify with his pupils at the expense of collaboration with his colleagues.

Teachers who experience a sense of powerlessness and irreconcilable conflict between their principles and their practice may try to protect themselves by withdrawing into the parochial security of their classrooms. One symptom of this is the frequent difficulty teachers have in talking to each other about their work, or in finding joint solutions to their problems. Consultation is not easy, and teachers are driven to operate in isolation from one another. In such circumstances there is bound to be an excessive concern with visible evidence of personal success. The awarding of marks and examination results will be given disproportionate importance, and will have invested in them a great deal more emotion than they deserve. Overtly the teacher may be concerned with the success of the children in realistic terms, but what is in fact at stake is rather the teacher's own security. Where the teacher feels that his status and career depend on the children's academic achievements, anything that is likely to interfere with these achievements will generate anxiety. He will tend to be most appreciative of those pupils whose behaviour in the classroom is orderly, silent and dependent. Any sign of disobedience or lack of concentration, even questions which divert the narrowly determined flow of the lesson, will be experienced as threats which must be eliminated. The teacher who is caught up in so limited a view of the nature of teaching may find it hard to bear the uncertainties associated with having students in his classroom. The autonomy of the teacher in the classroom is rightly valued, but there is a price to be paid.

Children in schools whose educative function becomes diverted by the overriding need to contain and control are likely to respond in one of three ways. First, they may submit to the authoritarian system of the school and apparently accept it; second, they may be overtly hostile and rebellious; and third, they may withdraw from it in one way or another.

The first response, of submission, may sometimes look like willing cooperation, but where there is no sharing of the responsibility for learning between teacher and taught it is more likely to be a negative than a positive response. To sit quietly at his desk and to do what he is told may represent the child's reading of what the authoritarian teacher and school want of him. This is probably the largest group in the classroom, and includes those able and resilient children who carry off the rewards the school offers. Much of their creative energy however will be absorbed in trying to guess what the teacher's intentions are: they will tend, for example, to give safe rather than adventurous answers, to write correctly rather imaginatively, to reduce every transaction in the classroom to a mechanical and ritualistic process. It is disturbing to consider that in schools of this kind such children are regarded as the most successful and are thought to justify the school's approach to learning. These are the children who become 'good citizens', but the emphasis on conformity will not have developed to the full the more creative aspects of their personality.

While it is true that the majority of children in school remain for the most part submissive to the demands made on them, there are a spirited few who try to preserve their individuality within the system. This may be expressed in different ways. It is, for example, characteristic of a paternalistic regime to allow a certain amount of hostility to be expressed in conventional ways. A teacher may tolerate or even encourage a joking relationship with some members of the class, who will use this as a means of giving vent to their hostility. Joking can be a socialized form of aggression and can add a dangerous and yet exciting dimension to the relationship with the teacher. The boy who takes part in recognized banter with the authoritarian teacher is walking a tightrope: representing the hostility latent in the class, he runs the risk of isolation from his peers if he incurs the teacher's displeasure, but he will enjoy considerable prestige if he can create the appearance of a relaxed atmosphere. Whichever way it goes, the class is once again more concerned with reading the signals from the teacher than with working. More obvious forms of hostility are also familiar and inevitable in the authoritarian school. They may be directed against the teacher, in the form of time-wasting and creating disturbances even to the extent of sabotaging the lesson, or against other children. Fighting in the playground, bullying and gang activity are common features of an authoritarian regime, and they in turn appear to the school to justify its repressive measures. In such a climate cooperation among children will find little place except when used as a weapon against authority. Where aggression cannot easily be shown openly it will be expressed in symbolic ways: thieving, destruction of school property, defacing of textbooks and writing on lavatory walls. Such activities represent an attempt on the part of this minority to bring the system to a standstill, and the authorities, as though sensing the symbolic intention of such spoiling tactics, tend to over-react. Physical violence against children and expulsion from school are still not infrequent and suggest an unthinking application of authoritarian values.

The third response that children may make is one of apathy and withdrawal. These children, who are unable to meet the formal demands of work handed out to them in a competitive framework, and at the same time are unable for reasons of personality to join actively in the social life of the class, have no alternative but to opt out. As they are not overtly hostile and sit quietly without disturbing other children they represent no threat to the authoritarian teacher, and are easily overlooked. Absenteeism is common among this group, not necessarily the colourful kind of truancy indulged in by more hostile children, but a quiet contracting-out. Even occasional absences can seriously interrupt school work: important sequences in learning are missed, assignments cannot be completed, and the strain resulting from this leads in turn to further absenteeism. Where there is competition and frequent testing this process of erosion is hastened. Such absenteeism is sometimes made easier because the school, recognizing that these children will have no success in the terms it offers, appears to condone it.

In order to highlight some of the difficulties of effective teacher training we have discussed how teachers and children may respond to schools with an excessively authoritarian structure. Such schools undoubtedly still exist, and to a greater or lesser degree teachers in many more are forced by the expectations that society has of them to act in authoritarian ways. The climate of opinion is changing and the old-fashioned martinet is less commonly found. In many ways, though, the structure of our schools appears to remain essentially unchanged, and under pressure they easily revert to repressive measures. For the most part young teachers will have no desire to be authoritarian, but they will find it very difficult to function with full effectiveness in such a setting. They are likely to have sympathy for children in the predicament we have described and indeed, as beginners themselves, have something in common with them. The very fact that they are not yet fully identified with the system means that they are often able to communicate easily with their classes and to produce lively and creative work with them. Too often though this work is done in isolation and is not recognized or appreciated by teachers who favour more formal methods. Encouragement of new approaches and of youthful enthusiasm does not come easily to teachers caught up in the scramble for conventional tokens of success.

When the young teacher is faced with less able children his task becomes even more complex. He may know at a rational level that the formal academic standards of the school and a competitive approach to learning are inappropriate, yet the resulting pressures on him will be difficult to ignore. Unsure of his status in the power structure of the school, and unconfident as yet of his ability to earn the respect of these particular children by his own worth, his very perception of them may well become distorted. If they fail to respond to his efforts he may very easily see them as hostile, ready to threaten what little authority he feels he has. If he himself experiences the authority structure of the school as potentially threatening he may well recreate a sort of mirror-image in his own classroom, supposing that children experience him in the same way. In an attempt to forestall any active expression of hostility he may resort to threats, unrealistic punishments and arbitrary behaviour inconsistent with his real personality. This will eventually arouse actual hostility in the class, and once this has happened and a sense of grievance has become rooted on both sides, any possibility of communication between the children and himself becomes more and more remote. Many young teachers of intelligence and ability can quickly become discouraged in such circumstances, and in self-defence may surrender to the prevailing values of the school. Such a surrender is made even more certain when, as often happens, a young teacher who has established friendly relationships with at least some of his pupils is warned off from becoming too familiar with them on the grounds that the teacher's authority depends upon the distance of formal relationships. There is in this whole situation an appalling waste of potential, both of teachers who wish to work in a sympathetic and responsible way and of children who can only learn from such an approach.

Most of the students in colleges and departments of education who become young teachers are by definition successful products of the existing school system. They have found satisfaction in academic work, have played for school teams, run school societies, and will often have been prefects or heads of house and school. Throughout their school careers they will have been grouped in top streams with children of similar aspirations and abilities, and it is unlikely that they will have had much to do with those children who form the majority of the school population. At home as well as at school they may have been actively discouraged from mixing with and running the risk of 'contamination' by such children. Many student teachers, having experienced success themselves, have a genuine wish to make sure that all children share in it too. They are often committed to liberal and progressive educational ideals. Yet they find it hard to believe that everyone is not motivated by the same carrots that were held out to them. When they encounter children whose goals and values are different from theirs, and whose pace and method of working are unfamiliar, they are often shocked and may feel themselves rejected. They find it hard to believe that their careful plans of work, based on approaches which have succeeded for them and arising out of a genuine concern for the children's learning, can be unacceptable. In any human situation when something is offered with generous intentions its rejection will give rise to anxiety and pain, which can easily turn to anger. In normal social situations of this kind the rejected one can often simply slam a door and walk away. The teacher cannot do this, and his anger is likely to lead to a breakdown of whatever constructive dialogue between himself and the children may have been established. Some teachers, after years of struggle and experience, achieve the imaginative insight to cope with the frustration and hostility which work with less able children entails. One of the problems of effective teacher training is to help the young teacher from the outset to draw upon his reservoir of sympathy and intelligence, which too often becomes inaccessible as a result of certain characteristics of his own upbringing and education.

The success students have experienced at school, college or university has been due in part to the support they have had from their homes. Most of them will be from social classes which unquestioningly accept the value of 'getting on' and which are prepared to postpone immediate satisfactions for the long-term interest. They will tend to be people who put a high value on ambition, initiative, good manners and an ordered life. Not that they will necessarily believe wholeheartedly in these values, but because they have often been maintained with difficulty and some self-sacrifice, they may tend to be critical of those whose lives are not governed by them. Most of the children who find themselves in the lower streams of secondary schools, whatever the intention of the selection procedures, are from working-class homes. A minority of them will get no support from their parents for their progress in school; others will have this support, but it will be limited by lack of knowledge and suspicion of the aims of the school. Such children will be conditioned to expect immediate rewards and punishment, will not be familiar with rule-dominated middle-class behaviour, and will be more likely to act on impulse than to consider the social consequences of what they do. Here are the makings of conflict between the young teacher and many of the children he will be called upon to teach. It should be added that even those students whose own background is working-class may be insufficiently secure in their new professional role to be able to sympathize with them easily.

A further limiting characteristic of the traditional education of most student teachers is that elitist view of culture which is common in schools and society alike. It may be that the student's struggle to achieve examination success has been at the cost of a more spontaneous and dynamic response to experience. There may have been little opportunity for developing personal and aesthetic interests – all will have been sacrificed to the need to meet the external demand of formal 'learning'. The student in this situation may have found it difficult to establish and keep alive a personal and genuine concern for a broadly based view of culture. There will often be reverence for the achievements of the past, but less commonly a dynamic interest in current artistic and intellectual development. Such a lack of interest may lead the teacher to be insensitive also to the creative potential of the children he teaches. Their expression of originality and initiative is often experienced as a threat in the classroom. The teacher who does not recognize the creative impulse as it appears in his interaction with children may feel so bewildered and made so anxious by its manifestations as to be driven to reject it altogether. This kind of energy has been mobilized in the best of our junior schools but, generally speaking, there is little evidence of it in secondary schools. There creativity is too often split off to the artroom and the weekly music lesson. The young teacher's genuine disappointment at the children's rejection of the cultural values he has to offer – which he may interpret as evidence of laziness, apathy or bloodymindedness – may merely reflect the narrowness of his own view of what culture can be. When the young teacher begins teaching he is usually ready to share his interests with his pupils, but all too often, when he is unable to make any lively response to the children's own culture, his interest can appear as remote and even condescending. It is not that the teacher should try uncritically to accept everything in the teenager's view of his world – in any case this is a self-defeating procedure – but that he should have sufficient respect for children and sufficient confidence in his own judgement to recognize what is of value in it. Only when a dialogue has been started through this approach can the teacher hope to relate what he values in his own cultural life to the needs and interests of the adolescent.

A somewhat similar situation may occur in the case of the student teacher who has specialized in a particular subject. Because of his commitment to it, his attitude towards this subject is often one of respect for its content and structure which he feels is, or ought to be, wholly within his grasp. When the children in the classroom do not at once join with him in this attitude there is again an area of potential conflict. His own experience of education may well have encouraged in him the belief that the teacher ought to be an infallible expert. A great deal of sixth-form and college and university teaching consists of the handing down of information and opinions, on the assumption that the learner is in a dependent relationship with the teacher. The student teacher, even if intellectually he wishes to break free from this pattern, when faced with the inevitable pressures of the classroom may understandably regress to the situation he is most familiar with. He may fall back on his subject as a major prop for his sense of security.

Such a response can have further effects, for a retreat into subject expertise may make it difficult for the young teacher to communicate easily with other teachers of the subject. He may feel that those more experienced than himself will think less of him for any admission of inadequacy, whether in classroom management or in grasp of his subject. Furthermore, his inexpertise in other subject areas may inhibit any exchange of ideas and experience with colleagues outside his own department. Where knowledge is seen as an end in itself, with an undue emphasis on the subject, it is difficult for the teacher to be sufficiently flexible to adapt to new approaches to learning. Team teaching, an integrated curriculum, interdisciplinary inquiry will all appear threatening because all such approaches demand a readiness to share ideals and take risks. Teachers of less able children in particular need to be sufficiently adaptable to plan and carry out these approaches, since for many such children the traditional subject-based curriculum is evidently inappropriate.

The whole experience of most student teachers, the encouragement they have had from their homes and the successes they have achieved at school, leaves them ill-equipped to regard objectively the system which has nurtured them. They are likely to be over-involved with the school as an institution, and will consequently find it difficult to conceive that it could be different. They may well be alert to particular absurdities in the system, but will rarely understand or be critical of its basic structure. They may, for example, criticize schools where boys have to wear caps, but will not think to question the institutional function of uniforms in general. This is hardly surprising since, partly because of the fragmentation of curricula in schools, colleges and universities, there is no encouragement given to questioning the objectives and functioning of the institutions themselves. The assumption is made that they have been arranged for the best of reasons and it is no business of pupils or students to question their inevitability. Current student and sixth-form unrest are a sign that this situation is changing, but young teachers will only be able to cope with changes and develop them constructively if they have some basic insight into the nature of institutions and their own experience of them.

We have laid emphasis on the difficulties which the young teacher may encounter in school. It is not that we are unaware of the rewards and successes which many experience from the beginning, but it seems important to spell out the sources of difficulties, to arrive if we can at better means of preparing teachers for them. In our experience most students who come into teaching come with the intention of being of use to the community at large. They have enjoyed the relative freedom of being students, with time to explore ideas, to follow through chosen areas of interest, and to use facilities for study which are easily accessible. Removed for the most part from the constraints of family life, they have been put in a position to organize their own lives with a comparative lack of restriction. This independence has helped them to be more conscious of the needs of others and relatively confident in their ability to meet new situations effectively. They are willing to give generously of time and effort to learn the skills of their chosen profession. Faced with the necessity of earning a living in a respectable, regulated and responsible job, however, it is not surprising that they sometimes find it difficult to reconcile the freedom they have enjoyed with the desire to be useful to the community. Their attitudes both to vocationally directed education courses and to the practical orientation of schools are likely to be ambivalent. They need sympathetic help to face this feeling of ambivalence if they are to tolerate the necessary restraints of a professional job without feeling that they have betrayed their student ideals. If this transition is not handled carefully on education courses and in schools the student may well abandon his ideals and in the classroom may merely emulate uncritically whatever models of teaching are to hand.

To be really effective he has to create for himself a way of teaching which works but which is in accord with his idealism, and to do this he will need considerable support both as a student and in his first years as a teacher. One source of conflict for the young teacher, for instance, is the amount of routine necessary for a school to function properly. He may feel any routine to be an imposition on his freedom of action, and be reluctant to reconcile himself to the administrative requirements of the job. He has to learn to evaluate the demands made upon him by the administrative routine of the school, recognizing what is essential and living with what is not, until he is in a position to change it. He will also have to deal with the fantasies which abound in schools as in all other institutions. His relative isolation as a newcomer may give rise in him to unreal fears that he is totally without power and unable to take any initiatives. He may be afraid to approach the head or older teachers, who might well be only too prepared to help him. His inexperience may lead him to have exaggerated fears that any minor disorder in his classroom will inevitably lead to chaos. These fears are made worse by the common assumption that any failing, however trivial, will be observed and recorded by the head on whose good testimonial his future depends. Such fantasies can only be managed when the young teacher is enabled to acquire some measure of objectivity, either by hard experience or through a more effective professional training.

Essentially, what is required is that all the parties to teacher training – the students, the teacher trainers and the teachers in schools – should be brought together in a realistic and clearly defined working relationship. The theory and practice of education must be more closely related, and the roles of supervisor and teacher in school clarified. The unconscious anxieties which give rise to the 'school-practice game' need to be explored, so that both sides can work more effectively for the student's development. The student must be helped to value his own experience, yet be sufficiently detached from it to adapt what he knows to the needs of all the children he will meet in the new secondary schools. He can only learn to act effectively and with true authority in the classroom on the basis of an understanding of his own role and the nature of the institution within which he is working. Without this knowledge the pressures to fall in with the unthinking authoritarianism of schools at their worst will be overwhelming. This in turn has implications for teacher training. It is vital that the student's experience of his professional education should be of a genuinely participatory kind. It is not enough for education courses to recommend non-authoritarian approaches to teaching, assuming that the mere recitation of a magic formula will have lasting effects. A genuine dialogue must be set up between tutors and students within colleges and departments of education, and between both these and teachers in schools.

Chapter 2
The Hillview Project:
An Approach to Teacher Training

We have described some of the obstacles which stand in the way of effective teacher training. We turn now to a scheme, the Hillview project, which was designed to help some of our students to meet the challenge of teaching the more 'difficult' children they would encounter in comprehensive schools.

Such children, often though by no means always the less able, tend to find school unrewarding and the efforts of their teachers irrelevant. It seemed to us that if students were to deal effectively with such children at all they must get to know them as part of their training in situations outside the normal school setting – where stereotypes on both sides operate so easily. The traditional forms of teaching practice may be inadequate for this purpose: the sudden confrontation of a student with the whole class may keep him so busy just surviving that he will learn comparatively little about the children as individuals. It seems to us that teaching practice, essential though it is, has to be supplemented by informal contacts with individual children or with very small groups. On the Hillview project we arrange every year for twelve students to work with a class of early school leavers in a comprehensive school on a working-class estate just outside a large city. These twelve students are recruited each year out of a group two or three times that number who have volunteered to take part in the project. The selection is made in a fairly arbitrary manner, though we attempt to include an equal number of men and women. Each student is attached to two or three children on every Wednesday afternoon throughout the academic year. The students are free to use the time in any way they wish. They can, for example, meet the children outside the school altogether, and in fact most of them choose to do so. The first aim of the project is to help the students to get to know the children in their groups. Each student is required to keep a journal describing and interpreting the events of the afternoon. Once a week the whole student group meets with us as tutors for discussion, and with the class teacher when he can come.

At the preliminary tutorial discussion, which is mostly administrative in function, we tell the students about the arrangements for meeting the boys and girls at the school. The class teacher allocates children to students, in friendship groups as far as possible, putting boys with men and girls with women when that can be done. The students are at this stage curious, and apprehensive perhaps, about how their first encounter with the children will go. From then on the situation in the tutorials grows more complex, for the students begin to acquire experience which we as tutors do not share. We do not see the students with their children and so must rely for our information upon their reports. This is very different from the traditional pattern of teaching practice, where the supervisor sits in on the student's lesson and by his very presence tempts him, however unconsciously, to adjust his behaviour to what he supposes the supervisor wants. Furthermore, through this direct surveillance, the student's capacity for insight into his own actions and for an independent evaluation of his own progress may well be diminished. The Hillview project puts considerable responsibility upon the students, and the fact that we are not present at the encounters between them and the children means that we are of necessity extremely cautious about any advice we give. We certainly cannot give advice or make any comment *until* the student himself has described what has happened. We have tried to avoid shaping the experience of each new group of students by reference to what has happened in earlier years. We have rather, where comment has been called for, referred to relevant literature or to our own experience with children in other circumstances. Of course any student in particular difficulties has been supported, but this has usually been a matter of helping him to work out for himself what attitude or action he should adopt. For instance, on one occasion when the child was rumoured to be stealing we tried, in group discussion, to help the student to sort out the nature of any teacher's responsibility to a child, to the parents, to the school and to the community at large. It was left to him to draw the conclusions.

Our role as tutors can in a sense be described as non-directive, and we use this term when we talk about our method of supervising the group. From what we have said already about our interaction with the students it is clear that this term does not mean 'unpurposeful' or 'anarchic'. In the introductory session when the project is outlined to the students our aims are set out in what we hope are clear terms of reference: to give students some insight into the lives and problems of 'difficult' children, through working with them in small groups over an extended period outside the structure of the school curriculum. We explain our hope that the intensity and continuity of the experience will lead to a deeper understanding of the children and of the students' interaction with them. We make one absolute condition in asking for volunteers, that however painful the experience and however difficult the children, no student has the right to contract out of the project. We want to make it quite clear that the project is not an academic exercise – it involves commitment to real children, some of whom will certainly have experienced persistent rejection by adults whose expectations they have not been able to meet. We underline too that the project will put the student into a one-to-one or one-to-two relationship with the children and that, apart from learning about the children in their care, they can well be of real practical help to a child who might never before have had such concentrated attention from a caring non-parental adult.

Because of the rather general nature of our explanations the non-directive approach creates some difficulties. Our unwillingness to give advice at the level of the particular leads to students sometimes accusing us of giving them no advice at all – in fact a number of them have been under the impression that we have expressly forbidden them to engage in any kind of purposeful activity with the children. It is perhaps not surprising that many students are unable to 'hear' our initial explanations, partly because they are anxious at embarking on a new experience and partly because their education has so far involved only the successful negotiation of closely structured situations provided by their schools and universities. It is a further aim of the project, which obviously we cannot state to students at the outset, that they will learn through the constructive tensions engendered by a non-directive approach a valuable variation upon the more traditional teaching methods which most of them have been exposed to up to this point.

As tutors we have become aware of some of the dangers involved in such a teaching method: our interest in the behaviour of the group sometimes tempts us away from the real purpose of the meetings. We may sometimes hold back from comment almost as if we wish to see what might happen. The students on their part bring to the group their own feelings about authority, and sometimes react against us because we will not behave according to their expectations. They may ask us outright for directions which we cannot give or, particularly at the beginning, they may decline to talk about difficulties, not only for fear of losing face but as a means of forcing us to intervene. Frequently, though, any interventions we do make in the way of questions, comments or reference to relevant research are ignored by the students. They sometimes wish to blame us for a situation which makes them anxious or resentful. In order to justify such resentment they may invent the myth that we are completely inactive and enjoy chaos. A further threat to the group's successful operation arises from the fact that students are well aware that we as tutors have meetings of our own and have a professional interest in the whole field of educational deprivation. This knowledge sometimes makes them suspicious and engenders the fantasy that we may be merely using them for our own advancement. (There is an element of reality here of course: all teachers are in a sense 'using' their students – if only as a means of earning a living.) These suspicions may be one of the causes of some of the refusals to accept our interpretations of events under discussion. Accusations that we are letting our imaginations run away with us (for example, when we suggested that a girl whom someone described as a nymphomaniac might in reality be simply searching for affection and security), openly expressed resentment against us as individuals and, in contrast, occasional complete silence – these are all ways in which students express their ambivalence towards us.

One of the main problems students encounter with their children is absenteeism, and there are times too when they imitate the children's pattern of behaviour by staying away from the group tutorial, leaving early or arriving so late that no useful contribution can be made. In the absence of conventional leadership the group finds among its own members those who play the parts which might have been expected of us. In one year, for example, one student became the 'conscience' of the group, hectoring the others and by giving detailed accounts of his own successful activities demoralizing those who felt that they were not making that sort of progress. Similarly, each group has its victim. It seems as though, finding it difficult sometimes to manipulate us, they turn on one of their own members, whose only defence is to fill with idle and superficial talk what could have been useful contemplative silences. In such instances we find that the talk in no way matches the individual's normal level of intelligence and sensitivity, and we can only suppose that the whole process is unconsciously designed by the group as a means of avoiding real work. Not unnaturally these strains in the working of the group sometimes make us anxious, particularly when absenteeism is at its worst. Our regular discussions with one another help us to cope with these strains and allow us the luxury of letting the students express their feelings openly. We find that when such open expression of negative feeling can be tolerated and worked through, the relationship between tutor and group becomes in the end more realistic and work-centred.

It is important to realize that negative reactions like the ones we have described are characteristic of any working group. We have spent time discussing them here not because they are by any means dominant in the meetings, but because lack of acknowledgement and understanding of them can lead to unwarranted fears about a non-directive approach to teaching. Whatever our fears and fantasies, the meetings do continue, even the most hostile of silences ends. By not allowing the students to be dependent on our expertise and opinion we force them to draw on their own resources and work through their difficulties realistically. As many of them are people with creative energy, resilience and humour, committed to working with educationally deprived children, they are often able to mobilize these resources more readily than they might do in a conventional teaching situation. As time goes on they find us less threatening, their sense of their own potentiality becomes stronger, and they often develop in their ability to interpret their behaviour and that of the children. Over a year many of them arrive at a relationship which is highly personal, in which feelings are openly acknowledged, but which includes an awareness that factors such as the child's environment or past experience affect his behaviour at every point. This realization lends perspective to the student's view of himself in relation to the child, and frees him from a simple belief that he has either succeeded or failed in his relationship with him. This is the root of the proper conduct of a professional teaching relationship. It is part of the responsibility of teacher trainers to help their students as far as they can towards an understanding that this relationship entails a committed detachment, where behaviour towards the other person is warm and not impersonal, but at the same time is task-oriented and not self-indulgent. If, for example, a student reports an outburst of anger against a child, he is not encouraged to play it down but urged instead to ask himself the reason for his anger. The fact that tutorial discussions always take place some time after the students have been with the children means that the heat is off, they have had time to reflect and are more ready to discuss what has happened fairly dispassionately.

Naturally some students seek us out individually for private discussion when they are excited, pleased or worried over the turn of particular events. We find that we can distinguish here between two kinds of approach: occasions when a student feels insecure in the group and wants private support from us, and others where the group tutorial seems an inappropriate forum either for reasons of confidentiality or because some practical step has to be taken quickly. In one case a student came to us in great agitation because the boy in his charge had been committed to a remand home, and he did not know what he ought to do about it. In private discussion we were able to calm him down, put what had happened in some sort of perspective and, over the telephone, arrange on the spot for him to visit the boy.

Perhaps one of the most valuable elements in the help we are able to give students is in drawing their attention to the kinds of services that exist for children in trouble – and to do it at a time when it really matters to them. Although we give individual help when it is appropriate, it seems to us important that such matters should be discussed with the group as a whole, because it would be wrong to set up an individual relationship at the expense of the responsibility of the whole group to create an environment where all can work together. It is remarkable that though there is often shyness on the part of students who have approached us individually, they all, however reluctantly, do bring their problems before the group, often transforming initial anxieties into rational and considered judgement. This happens often enough without any questioning or prompting from us.

As in all professional relationships the problem of confidentiality is a major preoccupation of our students, and brings a number of them to us at different times for individual consultation. It seems to them at first that, because they are involved with the children and receive their confidences, there are matters which cannot be discussed before the whole group. What we have to demonstrate is that their professional role demands that they put to the best use whatever information comes their way about the children in their care. Of course the decision whether or not to tell us and the group of anything that has happened rightly remains with the individual. It could hardly be otherwise. There will certainly be occasions when a child's confidence must be respected absolutely. All teachers are faced with decisions of this kind of course, particularly in their pastoral function. How far they are able to share what they know with their colleagues in the certainty that it will be used constructively will depend on the kind of trust that has been built between them and higher authorities. Unfortunately in too many schools 'confidentiality' seems to mean the suppression of important information about children's problems. Those at the top of the hierarchy unconsciously create an illusion of power and omniscience for themselves, while those lower down never learn to use such information as comes their way at other than an anecdotal level. We recall an instance where a teacher had charge of a group of 'difficult' early school-leavers in a very traditional school, where each class teacher had been given strict instructions to see that all children were dressed in school uniform. There was one girl who was not dressed in uniform, and who would not say why. The headmistress was asked if there was any particular reason why special consideration should be given to that particular girl and her reply was, 'No reason at all, go ahead.' The girl was formally rebuked, to her distress, and a distraught mother arrived at the school the next day. For the first time the class teacher learnt – what she could have been alerted to before – that the girl's father was out of work, the mother kept a large family on next to nothing, and clothed all the children in cast-offs. The girl wet the bed every night and had to wash her sheets every morning before coming to school. This surely was an occasion when confidential information should have been made available to everyone concerned. It seems to us that over the year our students become more aware of how what they learn about the children can be discussed usefully with others. They themselves can learn from such discussion and can advance in their relations with the children. They become more detached, less sentimental, and in many cases become more able to respond to the children not at a conspiratorial level, but with an informed sympathy that helps both sides to deal realistically with the issues that arise in their relationship.

However, the issue of confidentiality can never be disposed of: it pervades all this kind of work, and the difficulties it creates and the anxieties it arouses should not be underestimated. In the Hillview project there is the further complication of confidential written material in the students' journals, as well as transcripts of tape-recorded conversations with the children. We believe that the journals, involving as they do a more reflective commentary on the students' interaction with the children than is possible in discussion, are a most important contribution to this work with teachers in training. We make it clear from the beginning that commitment to the project includes the students' writing up of their meetings with the children week by week. This is evidently not an easy task and quite a few of the students find it particularly onerous. We discuss the difficulties with the group: partly it seems ordinary indolence, partly a feeling that talking about their meetings is sufficient, partly, we suspect, a reluctance on these students' part to commit themselves to a reflective consideration of what they have achieved. Be that as it may, we also require that the journals should be shared amongst the members of the group, and from the start it is clear that each student has free access to what others have written. Amongst other difficulties that of confidentiality has to be coped with once again. For most it is; as students realize that exploring feelings and interpreting events through the written word has a value of its own, the quality of the journals often improves. The students are writing not only for themselves but for an audience of tutors and colleagues, and this sharing process perhaps helps them to sharpen their perceptions. As the year progresses they may learn better to trust us and one another, and move closer to an understanding of what their professional task is: to use what they know humanely yet unsentimentally for the benefit of the particular children they are dealing with, and so to improve their professional competence as teachers of other children in the future.

We have no doubts at all about our part in all this: we are engaged in teacher training, in helping a group of students to learn as much as possible about their professional role, especially when faced with the challenge of teaching children with whom most will have had little contact before. We find though that students often remain unsure about our motives. They find it difficult to accept that our non-directive approach does not imply lack of concern or idle curiosity. They have been brought up in an educational system where the habit of competition has driven them into the suspicious attitude that to share ideas with anyone else is to give them away without due reward. We suspect that this may be one reason for some students' taciturnity in discussion throughout their education course, even where the competitive factor has been reduced to a minimum.

We have described the functions of the students' journals – writing by its very nature encourages reflection upon the experiences presented by each individual. The kind of discussion which goes on in the group tutorials has rather different characteristics from the written accounts. Most importantly, discussion involves the participation of more than one person. In this case experiences are recounted before a sympathetic audience. This sharing of anecdotes about our experience, which others by their immediate response help us to modify in the interests of better understanding, is an important human activity and indispensable to the effective learning of any group. On some occasions the same story will be repeated several times over. This tends to happen particularly in relation to some disturbing incident – in one case a child had been seen by his student stealing from a shop. It was as though the group needed to hear this story several times as a means of assimilating its implications.

There are other important features of such a group-tutorial situation which the tutor has constantly to keep in mind. Sometimes, for instance, he may accept apparent frivolity which may be used to avoid more serious discussion too painful at the time for the group to bear. On occasions of this kind the painful topic, though laughed away at its first appearance, may be picked up seriously later in the session – picked up perhaps *because* it has been allowed to drop at first. The group has had time to prepare its defences. Another evident feature of this sort of discussion is the silence which from time to time overtakes the group. The tutor has to learn to interpret its nature. Is it solemn? Is it thoughtful? Is it an expression of grief or shock? Has it become threatening? He can only know at what point, if at all, to break it if he is sensitive to its meaning. Because the group has a work task and because we are responsible for ensuring that learning does take place we cannot remain entirely neutral, but necessarily assume a certain kind of leadership. We have to decide whether the group is working successfully, and if not whether it can be brought back to the task either by a simple redirection in terms of content or by turning the group's attention to the internal conflicts that divert it from its work. Sometimes, for example, it helps to draw attention to feelings of hostility towards ourselves which appear to be holding up the proceedings. From time to time the fact that we are making notes of what is said seems not unconnected with the group's temporary difficulty in talking freely. When we have referred to this possibility openly it has seemed to help the group to overcome its (very understandable) hesitation, and so to facilitate the flow of discussion.

Interventions in the area of content are more frequent. We always draw attention to the occasions when the group seems to deny the seriousness of issues which it has itself introduced to the discussion. Problems such as truancy, illiteracy or haphazard job-selection are sometimes referred to and instances of them described without any open expression of concern for the children involved. We know that many of the students become fond of particular children and accept them as the individuals they are, yet somehow they seem almost to accept as well the conditions of the children as they find them. An instance of this is the absenteeism which is quite common among some members of the class. Students learn through getting to know the children how deeprooted this is, and of course they themselves suffer from it. It is not unusual in some instances for children to fail to turn up for meetings on Wednesday afternoons. We are always surprised at how reluctant students are to take effective action about this. It would be very simple for them to insist on meeting their children at the school instead of at a distance from it and we urge them to do this whenever there is any difficulty about attendance. But almost always they prefer to go on making elaborate arrangements, exchanging letters with the children and so on, which seems almost designed to ensure confusion. Similarly, truancy is often referred to humorously in the group discussions. It is as though the undoubted commitment of students to the children in their charge remains in some respects at a personal but not a professional level. This is partly no doubt because of the limited nature of the Hillview project itself. Some of the problems the students become aware of cannot be even partially solved by them during their initial training year. This is a source of irritation of course to some of the 'activist' members of the group. Others may think – with some justification no doubt – that truancy is justified, that school itself or even their interventions, offer little enough of substance to these children. It also seems to us though that, having raised the issues, the students have sometimes then affected indifference as a means of protecting themselves against over-involvement. In rather the same way, some of the tough talk in school common rooms may be defensive in origin. However, what begins as understandable self-protection can only too easily become virtual indifference, and we see it as one of the functions of the tutorial group to help its members to tolerate the strong feelings which work with the less privileged will always arouse.

A further element of the contribution we are sometimes able to make to the tutorial discussions is reference to relevant theoretical or empirical studies. A major difficulty in education courses, as we have already described, is to marry theory and practice in the thinking of the intending teacher. Lecture courses are given, reading lists distributed, students encouraged to discuss their new learning in groups of various kinds and to write essays or examinations, yet the difficulty remains: for many students their studies in educational theory are still obstinately divorced from their practical work with children in

the classroom. The Hillview project makes it possible sometimes to relate theoretical work directly to ongoing practical
situations, whether it is Yablonsky's analysis of violent gangs,
or Bernstein's work on language and social class, or Goffman's
theorizing about the nature of institutions. It is not merely
that such theorists sometimes have direct relevance to some
particular situation exercising the group. Perhaps equally importantly, it may encourage students to conceive of themselves
as operating in a field that occupies the attention of a whole
range of professional workers. It is only through some such
awareness of the professional nature of their work that teachers
can acquire the detachment to make tolerable and effective the
passionate concern that work with young people demands.

We have tried to give some indication of the nature of our
work with students on the Hillview project, emphasizing the
negative as well as the positive aspects of it – all teaching
includes both. Success is always only partial, and in this kind
of enterprise impossible to assess with complete objectivity. We
think though that there is evidence that students increase their
understanding both of the young people they meet and of
themselves. We should like to finish with a postscript which one
of our students wrote after the completion of her year. She
attempted to evaluate what the year had done for her and to
explore the nature of the relationship she had built up with
Marilyn and Pat, the two girls in her charge. Perhaps she would
have demonstrated equal intelligence and sensitivity even had
she not taken part in the project. But at the very least we can
claim that it gave her the opportunity.

In some sense of course the 'scheme' has not ended for any of us.
I feel I have learnt a great deal from it which will be directly useful
in teaching, and one hopes that the children may have been encouraged to think about a few things which without us would have
escaped their notice. And for me there is the added fact that thanks
to her class teacher something more may be done about Marilyn's
hearing – he has spoken to her mother about it and has promised to
get her ears treated again. The question now is whether it will in fact
be too late for her to decide to stay on at school after all: I hope

that she does stay because she has such a definite interest in the kind of things that are taught at school that I'm sure she would profit from another year. What she would be best to do afterwards, I don't know. Would she enjoy office work as much as working in a factory? I don't know. I would recommend the extra year for its own sake rather than as a means to a 'better' job.

Beyond these questions, there are personal relationships. I have grown fond of Marilyn and as far as I can tell she is fond of me. I see no reason to end our relationship – it has already occasionally outgrown the bounds of Wednesday afternoons, and I shall see her again when I come back here in July. I hope that during the coming year she will come and stay with me – is this an unrealistic idea? Would a week in my middle-class suburban surroundings be so alien to her own world that it would have nothing to say to her? I think that the main value in it, apart from the fact that we should see each other again, would be simply that she would broaden her experience. It is easy for someone like me with the help of projects like this to enter homes of children like Marilyn, but it is less easy for these children as they grow up to move out of their own milieu: there is a wide gulf between the opportunities of those who go away to university and thereafter travel all over the place and those who get jobs as near as possible to their own homes and remain there. It is not a question of value but of choice. Those who travel and see all kinds of jobs and people might just as well decide that they would like to settle in their home towns and pursue the same career as their fathers and grandfathers – but at least this is their own decision. What 'educationally deprived' children seem to lack is the power to choose.

And yet odd weeks in new places will not alter this. What a few days staying with me could do for Marilyn is help her to develop her self-confidence: she would be seen by my friends as a person in her own right, not as part of a family, and she would have to speak for herself – something she enjoys doing and does not get much chance to do at home, where her mother, like so many mothers, is inclined to answer for her. She would have some new things to think about and talk about, and I think she would enjoy it, especially as her holiday this year is going to be a week at the sea with her parents – which she is looking forward to, but which will not, I think, bring her into contact with many new people.

And then there is Pat. I went to visit her (in the unmarried mothers' home) on Friday to collect a book I had lent her – she found it harder to talk to me than to chat to Marilyn and Christine, but she was quite friendly and seemed pleased to see anyone from outside the home. Her baby was due that very day, and she was in the home so that they can adopt it for her if she decides that she doesn't want to keep it. She will go to hospital to have the baby and then return to the home for some weeks, so I should be able to visit her there next month. The most encouraging thing that she told me was that her ten-year-old brother had been missing her: when she'd gone home for a few days he'd said: 'Next time, Pat, come back for real.' (I was interested that in recounting this to me she interpreted the words 'for real' in case I didn't know the phrase.) Another interesting point about the home itself is that they don't allow men visitors except the girls' fathers – one can see that there might be difficulties if gangs of boyfriends wanted to come, but it seems a bit unnatural for the girls to spend anything up to about five months shut away without seeing any men at all (except doctors and, when they go shopping, patients from the near-by mental hospital). I should have thought she could have been allowed to talk to my boyfriend for half an hour.

The difficult thing about Pat's situation, of course, is the fact that she will go home to the same friends, the same surroundings; and I don't see what chance she will have of starting afresh. She has at the moment no idea of what kind of job she wants, and unless she keeps the baby it seems to me of first importance that she should find a job in which she can take a real interest.

And so there are no conclusions. We have tried to evaluate our Wednesday and Friday meetings. The relationships are indeed strange because both manipulated (unlike a chosen friendship) and free (not altogether a working relationship: at least not, perhaps, ostensibly). There are definite affinities between these relationships and the 'group behaviour study' which also takes place in the course: people meet with a task, and yet the task is a close part of their relationship – the role of the student is similar to that of teacher and doctor, and yet the aim is to study rather than to act on the result of study. This apparent 'aimlessness' is one of the causes of depression and cynicism about the project and is quite natural since from early childhood we are used to working towards a set goal. (Future generations may be less rigid than we are if they are taught by heuristic methods.) It was also the cause of the tirade against the project uttered by a visiting lecturer. What he failed to realize was that action is of little use without thought: three years at university and one education year may seem to be a criminal waste of time if one is not pursuing a vast scheme of social work at the same time, and yet it is useless and dangerous to dabble in 'social reform' before one has studied history, people, society. At one time I wanted to be what was then known as an 'almoner' and I was shown round a London hospital by a medical social worker; she told me not to do a degree in social administration since it 'pigeon-holed' people too early, but to read English, French or History. I have mentioned this here because I think we are in danger of making 'social work' a too rigid process and underplaying the personalities of the people involved. 'Social creativity' is a very dangerous concept: words are dangerous enough as a medium without starting on people, and work with people requires a large measure of humility and an equally large amount of discussion about aims. Of course it is right that schoolchildren and students should be involved in work for their community, and conversely our learning will not stop when we become qualified teachers, but action has an insidious way of becoming a substitute for thought.

The Hillview tutorial meetings have sometimes seemed trivial, frustrating and useless. But perhaps one of the most important things I have learned this year is that this kind of frustration is not only necessary but also positive: it emphasizes, if nothing else, the difficulties inherent in coming to any conclusions about motives, inner feelings, relationships. We have learned something about how the children behave, think and feel, and we hope that we have broadened their experience a little. And we have learned about the mechanisms of society – detention centres, children's homes and so on – which we may have to contend with as teachers. We have learned that there are no obvious answers to the problems we shall meet. Perhaps we haven't done much for *these* children, but one hopes that we shall be able to do a little more as teachers, over a longer period.

Chapter 3
Five School Leavers

The Hillview project involves students over the course of a year in a relationship with children which exposes them, in some measure at least, to the fullness of the children's personality. They cannot help becoming aware of a wider range of children's lives and attitude than is easy for the busy classroom teacher. Inevitably there is a tendency in the school setting for teachers to see their pupils in a fragmented way. They are seen as learners of Biology or History, as disrupters of classroom discipline or as potential prefects, or as coming from 'good' or 'bad' homes. The very nature of the teacher's task encourages this partial view. He is concerned to foster development in particular directions, intellectual or social, in his pupils' becoming rather than their being. Children sense this partial view of their personality; some are able to meet the teacher's requirements successfully and are relatively unaffected by this fragmentation. But those who have little or nothing to offer to the specific demands of the teacher are likely to respond negatively to the whole school situation. The reluctant learners we are considering here are peculiarly vulnerable in this respect. They, even more than the successful children, need to be appreciated as the complex individuals that they are. Without this appreciation they can learn little or nothing from the school and must rely on the world outside it for their education. If school is to be made meaningful to them the teacher must open himself to the complexity of the children's experience of their own world. However narrow, unexciting or 'deprived' the lives of the Hillview children may seem to the outsider, they are in fact for the most part varied, absorbing and meaningful. Although for immediate purposes it is sometimes necessary to isolate specific aspects of the child's behaviour, it is vital that the teacher preserves a sense of the child as a whole person. To know that a particular child is partially deaf, for instance, may help to explain a good deal about his school work, but there will always be other aspects of his personality which the teacher must include in his view of him.

It is now generally recognized that teachers would sometimes be helped in understanding the learning problems of the children they teach if they paid visits to their homes and families. The difficulties of doing this in a natural and unobtrusive way are great and our students were fortunate that the extended relationship with their children made it relatively easy for them to see them in their home surroundings. Many of them were invited to meet parents and relations; Miss Angell describes such a visit in her journal from which the following extract is taken. She met the two girls for the first time in October.

Wednesday 12 February. Shirley invited Una and me to tea at her home in answer to my suggestion that she should decide what we were going to do this week. I arrived at about twenty to three and was met off the bus by Shirley and Una. We trotted round to their house – Shirley dragging along a rather reluctant dog and talking excitedly all the way. Inside, the house was rather dilapidated and tatty and filled with junk – though it was obvious that some rapid clearing up had been done in my honour, as piles of magazines and various bits and pieces had been stuffed under and behind armchairs. Although the place was tatty there obviously wasn't any shortage of money. There was a huge gramophone and television (twenty-three inch screen, as I was told!), with a large electric fire belting out heat at a phenomenal rate.

Shirley's mother was very pleasant, though she was obviously a little ill at ease at first. She was quite interested in what I was doing but was far more concerned to tell me what a gay life she led! This involved looking at hundreds of photographs showing 'me marrying our dad' to 'me getting drunk at Brighton'.

She was obviously very fond of her two little sons who were very quiet and shy at first – but she was unable to cover up the friction that exists between her and Shirley. For example, Shirley spilt some of her tea in her saucer and got a very sharp telling-off for her lack of manners! But when one of the boys tipped a whole cupful all over the carpet his mother found it highly amusing. Shirley was quick to point out the difference in her attitude towards her.

Both Shirley and her mother are very quick-tempered, over-critical and rather petulant. Obviously they are too much alike to get on well together. They were constantly correcting each other and getting impatient with each other. My presence acted as a restraint and Shirley's mother was obviously trying not to lose her temper with her or to give me a bad impression of their relationship. However, Shirley was aware of this also and refused to play the game!

At about 3.30 Mrs Jenkins left to go to work. She kissed the two boys before going and then on a sudden inspiration decided to kiss Shirley also! Shirley's reaction was '' 'ere, what you doing – you've never done that before – go away!' Obviously she felt her mother was being rather a fraud and did her best to thwart her attempts.

After her mother had gone Shirley came into her own right! She became rather excited and boastful and started to boss the two boys around. When the little one wet his pants both Una and I were rather surprised at the vehemence of her reaction. She shoved him out of the room very harshly, complaining bitterly and hitting him hard. She obviously resents very much having to look after the two boys so much and also her mother's preferential treatment of them. Accordingly she feels very little affection for them and treats them much as her mother treats her. It's a bit of a vicious circle as apparently Shirley's eldest brother is always hitting her, and she dislikes all her brothers to quite an extent.

All this time Una was sitting on the settee looking bored and giving me an occasional conspirational wink! She obviously wished to imply that this wasn't her idea of a rave.

I quite enjoyed the afternoon – surprisingly enough! Seeing Shirley with her family in this way gave me quite an insight into her behaviour and attitudes – her family are all rather nice, it's just that as a unit they don't work very well.

This visit to Shirley's home added another dimension to the picture of the child that Miss Angell was already building up in her journal. Here are some of her early impressions of Shirley:

I was greatly struck by her childlike appearance as she stepped off the bus. She was dressed in her best clothes as she willingly informed me. These consisted of a pink dress and a coat with a frilled collar, long white socks and black-heeled patent shoes. She is short and slim and physically immature.

Shirley was a very earnest and humourless little girl ... the prospect of different excursions does not seem to interest her.

Early on in the relationship Miss Angell recognized that there was some sort of antagonism between the girl and her mother. She evidently had a good deal of responsibility in the home for housework and for looking after her baby brother. It was apparent that Shirley would quite like to have stayed on at school, but her mother thought she should begin work as soon as possible. It seemed to the student that Shirley easily acquiesced to this as to everything else. To all appearances, both at school and in her relationship with Miss Angell, Shirley was quiet and unassuming, not given to any open expression of hostility. She seemed as a result not to have drawn attention to herself at school. Yet as time went on she revealed more and more of her real self and its complexity. Although she irritated Miss Angell at times, basically the relationship was a good one. Here on 29 October Shirley and Una are talking with her about smoking:

UNA: You don't smoke very much, do you, not really?

MISS ANGELL: About ten a day.

SHIRLEY (*surprised*): Last week you never smoked any!

MISS ANGELL: I didn't know whether I ought to – I didn't want to corrupt you (*both burst into laughter*) but as you are old hands I needn't have worried.

UNA: I gave them up four days ago – I always used to smoke for ages –

SHIRLEY: And me.

MISS ANGELL: How could you afford it?

SHIRLEY: Well you see, every morning I get ninepence a day – and then on Saturday I gets five bob. I used to sort of save that like during the week or till I got enough, then I used to get some.

UNA: And me.

MISS ANGELL: Not very many then.

SHIRLEY: About ten.

MISS ANGELL: Ten a week?

SHIRLEY (*very surprised*): No, ten a day!

MISS ANGELL: Ten a day! What were they? Number 6?

SHIRLEY: Yeh – I love them.

UNA: I used to – used to – get a packet of ten – then wait for my pocket money and get a packet of twenty – so I had them sort of to look back on.

SHIRLEY: Yeh – that's what I used to do. (*Both laugh.*)

MISS ANGELL: Where did you smoke them? Doesn't your mum mind?

SHIRLEY: My mother would kill me.

MISS ANGELL: Where did you smoke them then? On the way home from school?

UNA: I used to smoke them at home – my mother was hardly ever there, she goes out to work in the evening.

SHIRLEY: My mum is never home anyway – but of an evening I used to go out a lot and we used to meet down there round by the pub – we used to smoke them down there – we never used to worry about people going past.

Even though there may be some element of bravado here, Shirley is clearly able to talk frankly with the student about herself and her activities. It is interesting that both girls seem to accept without question that their mothers are not at home in the evenings. But in Shirley's case there was more to it than this. Her mother's relations with her seemed not merely neglectful but, at times, openly aggressive:

Wednesday 24 November. Shirley told me about an argument with her mother. She was very anxious to justify her point of view and obviously very greatly resented the way her mother had been trying to spoil her fun. Her mother had wanted Shirley to stay away from school on Wednesday morning to look after the baby so that she could go and have her hair permed. Shirley had refused – both of them had got very angry, the mother saying that Shirley was selfish and Shirley accusing her mother of the same. The mother grabbed Shirley by the hair and shook her violently, then stormed out of the house saying that she would not make an appointment for Shirley to have her hair done as she had promised. In fact she returned later and said that she *had* made an appointment for her. Shirley, whose feelings were still rather bruised, merely said, 'Yes.' The lack of gratitude incensed the mother and there was another scene which ended then with Shirley saying, 'You just wait till my dad comes home.'

Apparently Shirley's father feels that his wife favours the boys in the family at Shirley's expense. In turn Shirley feels that her resentment against her mother is justified, and told me gleefully how when her father did come home for dinner her mother was 'as sweet as pie'.

Up to this point Miss Angell is relying on Shirley's version of her relationship with her mother. According to her own words, she is the victim of her mother's neglect and aggression and in general she has given the impression of being 'a sad little creature'. It was not until Miss Angell was with the girl in everyday situations with other people that she saw her as a more complex individual. The Hillview project enabled the students to take the children to their own rooms or flats, where they often met the students' friends in an informal setting. (It is rarely that teachers or teachers in training have the opportunity to gain the insights which such a situation can provide.) On this occasion Miss Angell, who had had a rather quiet and depressing afternoon with Shirley, invited her home:

When we got back to the flat Shirley became aggressive, self-assertive and defensive – all at the same time! With me she is still a bit touchy about some things but is willing to confide in me and feels reasonably secure in my company. So, although it is perhaps good that she should mix with lots of other people, the immediate effects on her are not so good.

She started to attack Kevin – a friend of mine who read philosophy at university but chucked it in after two years and is now laying concrete in the centre of the town. Shirley said that he had wasted his time at university and what good was education if it did not help you to get a well-paid job. Kevin explained his views to her – that education was a good thing in itself and wasn't necessarily a means to a definite end. But Shirley insisted that nothing was worth doing unless it yielded more money!

The important thing about this is not Shirley's sense of priorities but the response which this conflict of ideas evoked in her. Kevin is a tremendously shy, gentle person and he was in no way attacking Shirley, but merely trying to explain his views to her. But Shirley refused to listen, insisted loudly that she had won the argument – 'I beat you there, didn't I?' – ridiculed Kevin and his ideas while at the same time feeling obviously rather unsure of herself. After Kevin had left she tried to find out what I thought by saying, 'I think it's daft – going to university just to work on the roads!' I explained that he had gone to university to learn what other men may have thought or written about life and its meaning – or lack of it – and Kevin had left in order to sort out his ideas. Shirley couldn't see that this was a particularly valuable thing to do, and obviously she could hardly be expected to when her own life was geared to getting out to work and earning her living. Thought is a luxury Shirley feels she can't afford.

Miss Angell was clearly taken aback by the unaccustomed display of aggression. It seems that Shirley was trying on an adult role, engaging in argument as her experience suggested adults did. Kevin had outraged all her feelings about education – he was voluntarily doing the sort of work which the boys she knew might well be forced into for lack of qualifications. As Miss Angell saw very clearly, Shirley's view of life could hardly embrace the notion of thought for its own sake. For the girl, as no doubt for her parents, education is seen as having a strictly utilitarian function (a view often reinforced by schools). She has little conception of the nature of rational discussion, but is restricted to a quarrelsome mode of argument. She can only respond to Kevin's kindly attempts to explain his way of life to her by seeing his non-conformist view of life as a personal attack on her. It is becoming clearer that despite her apparent listlessness Shirley is capable of strong feelings that she does not find easy to control.

To return to our first extract recounting Miss Angell's visit to Shirley's home, her growing awareness of the complexity of the child's life and personality is now given substance. Miss Angell sees that Shirley cannot get on with her mother, is desperately jealous of her brothers, and is given more responsibility for them than she can tolerate. As the result of actually having experienced the tensions in the family, Miss Angell is better able to understand the girl's behaviour in other situations. During the year the relationship with Shirley develops and deepens. This does not mean that it became easier, but both Shirley and Miss Angell were more able to be themselves. In the early stages of these relationships with the Hillview children all the students feared that any quarrels or disagreement would irrevocably damage the relationship they were trying to build up. By the end of March Miss Angell gives the following account of a row she had with Shirley:

Shirley shouted good-bye to me and commanded me in her usual self-righteous way not to forget to write to her this time. I wasn't aware of any occasion on which I had forgotten to write and I am afraid I saw red. I told her she had a bloody nerve – that for the past four weeks I had hung around the Union for half an hour or more waiting for her and she hadn't bothered to let me know that she wasn't coming – so she could damn well write to me for a change.

Not surprisingly Shirley was most affronted by this and stormed off, muttering darkly under her breath. I regretted losing my temper but I am no saint and that kid certainly knows how to rub me up the wrong way. Besides I don't think it would be a bad thing from the point of view of our relationship to have said this. I am getting a bit fed up with being taken so much for granted. All Shirley ever has to offer me is criticism and although I understand why she is always so much on the defensive and so self-righteous it's hard always to bear these things in mind. I expect she is quite fond of me in her own way – it is a shame she is not better at showing it! I suppose I'd better write to her and clear the air a bit.

Far from destroying the relationship between Miss Angell and Shirley, the row seems to have served to strengthen it. Miss Angell remains thoughtful and sympathetic about Shirley and Shirley draws closer to her, in the end talking to her about herself more openly than ever, about her conflict with her mother and about the extent of her duties at home, where she has only Saturday nights off – if she is lucky. She particularly took Miss Angell into her confidence over her relationship with the other members of her class:

She has relatively little pocket money and is very upset that she can't go camping with the rest of the class. Apparently Shirley's mother thinks it's a very bad idea for boys and girls to go camping together and one can understand her point of view. But it's also easy to see Shirley's – she says her classmates call her mammy's babby – if they can go camping why can't she?

Her classmates also call her names. She says that nobody speaks to her unless they want something – whereupon they promise not to call her names – but the minute she gives them what they want they revert to their former rudeness. She says that Una is the same – the only time she speaks to her is when they are with me.

Her words reveal a depth of loneliness that I had only guessed at before – the gaiety and chirpiness when with the rest of the class are obviously attempts to win their friendship – but she resorts to other methods as well. She is fond of spreading tales and eagerly spreads around any gossip that's going.

She is much less physically mature than the rest of the form. I remember when I first saw her, I thought she couldn't be more than twelve. This is an obvious disadvantage – girls of her age tend to be very figure-conscious and despise those poor creatures who are less well endowed with nature's gifts! The boys are the same – Shirley's sexlessness makes her a figure of fun and scorn. Unfortunately, she is so desperate to be like the others that she runs after any available male. She withstands all rebuffs, rudeness and scorn and mockery of other girls in her attempts to secure the affections of some eligible young man – whose self-consciousness invariably won't allow him to associate himself with such an object of ridicule.

The whole thing is just one big vicious circle. I don't think I can be of much help, except to lend a ready ear to Shirley's complaints and see if I can't help her to come to terms with herself a bit more. But certainly I see no point in forcing the child to *do* things on Wednesday afternoons – it's obviously of no benefit to her. If necessary we will sit in my flat every week drinking coffee and talking – maybe we'll get somewhere in the end.

Miss Angell is modest about how much help she could give Shirley, yet her sympathy, based on real understanding, can only be of benefit to a child who is unappreciated by almost all who come into contact with her. Certainly Miss Angell herself has achieved considerable insight into the complexity of a girl who had seemed a fairly unremarkable member of her class. Only gradually and over a long period of time, with frequent opportunities for informal contact, did this awareness develop.

The students' weekly meetings with the children were often difficult and exacting, particularly for those with children who appeared to be apathetic and were certainly inarticulate. The appearance of apathy is often seen by teachers in schools as symptomatic of laziness. Certainly the failure to respond to anything the teacher offers can be frustrating for him, and in a large group there are practical difficulties in the way of investigating the apparent apathy of individual children. The Hillview project gave some students the opportunity to begin to do this. Mr Ross writes of his first meeting:

Alf and Harold are both aged fifteen, both scruffy in appearance and both rather uncertain of themselves. Alf is particularly uncertain – he relies on Harold to answer questions and to volunteer information. .'. . 'Hey, Harold, what do you think?' Harold is taller with a certain leader-ability, he is school weight-lifting champion – having a well-proportioned frame. He is dark, warty, with an amateur haircut and nicotine-stained fingers. Alf is shorter and stockier, with long greasy fair hair and he tends to look up to Harold.

It quickly became clear to Mr Ross that he was going to have difficulty in finding activities that would interest the two boys. Whatever he did and however hard he tried they remained apparently indifferent and reluctant to commit themselves. As Mr Ross came to know more about the social background of the boys, he began to explore the nature of this response and to discover reasons for it. For one thing they seemed quite unable to take up opportunities offered to them to do anything new. At the end of October Mr Ross, after an attempt to interest the boys in an improvised folk-skiffle session, realizes that the problem is one of a general lack of interest:

They have little to be enthusiastic about – nothing much happens in Hillview, they probably can't afford to go to the city centre for entertainment; they have the prospect of a dead-end job and they spend most evenings either with their mates or at a club – I must accept their invitation to go there one evening. Their apathy is so ingrained that even when they have the opportunity to do something interesting their enthusiasm is infected with boredom.

Like many of the students, Mr Ross tried to meet the problem by engaging with the boys in a round of activity: visits to a skating rink, games of table-tennis, outings to the museum or amusement arcades. Although the boys enjoyed some of these activities, Mr Ross felt that he had accomplished little.

6 December. Another afternoon spent with absolutely no feeling of achievement. Having passed half an hour in a one-armed bandit hall we come back here to the art studio. The boys always enjoy themselves there although they do not necessarily do anything much. I feel we ought to be achieving something by now but we are not. It is the same old round of dirty cracks and youthful chatter.

The frustration Mr Ross feels is related to the relative superficiality of the relationship the boys have been prepared to enter into. They had been ready to tag along with whatever he suggested, but had never shown any enthusiasm or initiated any activity themselves. This was particularly true of Alf. At a Christmas party for all the children and students involved in the project these two boys were among the least able to participate. After a while Harold did join in, but Alf remained very much on the outside. This reluctance to participate became, on a later occasion, an outright refusal. Mr Ross had arranged with the boys, and with Alf's apparent approval, to go swimming at the Students' Union pool. When they arrived, however, Alf announced that he was not going to swim:

I asked him why and he said he didn't want to. Harold said Alf's mother wouldn't let him. I asked if it was because he couldn't afford it. No. Would he swim if I paid and we hired some trunks? No. He said it was because he had a cold that his mother forbade him. But Alf never looks you in the eye when he tells you white lies and I suspect there is more to it than a cold. However, I could see he was getting upset about my questions and being taunted by the other boys. So I took Harold swimming because Alf seemed very happy to retire to the balcony and watch. However I feel things are getting worse with Alf. He is never very keen on anything we do and always seems disconsolate. Later I again tried to talk to him but made absolutely no headway. He said he would not go swimming or ice skating next week but would be content to watch. I said I would pay for him if that was the trouble. He said no – it was just that he didn't want to participate. He prefers to watch. He is so difficult to communicate with.

The one encouraging development in the relationship was Alf's increased ability to explain his feelings. From an initial passivity, through stubborn opposition, he progressed to greater willingness to state his own point of view. This was only possible because Mr Ross persevered despite his frustration, refusing to give the boy up. Despite many occasions on which plans agreed with Alf had to be abandoned because of his subsequent opposition, Mr Ross continued in a friendly way to try to get him to understand his own inconsequentialities. On 19 February, after an apparently enjoyable game of snooker in the Students' Union, Alf declared that he would not be coming the next week because he was fed up and would rather stay at school. Mr Ross writes:

I was visibly put out by this information and set about finding his reasons. This was not easy because he can be very stubborn as well as inarticulate. I finally got him to admit that it was because we always did things in a crowd, with other groups. In retrospect I see Alf was always most forthcoming when there were just the three of us. Presumably because of his lack of self-confidence, he never stated any preference when I asked him where he wanted to go nor did he say that it should be just with me and Harold. But now that Alf has admitted his wishes I shall have to be more careful about what we do. He has agreed to come next week provided that we do not join with anyone else.

It often seemed to us that boys like this found it difficult to share their student with others. Maybe for many of them it was the first time they had had an opportunity for an extended friendly adult relationship outside their own family. Alf presented himself on the one hand as a typical member of his peer group, interested in pornographic literature, jokes and songs or absorbed by a display of Nazi paraphernalia in a shop window; he wore a Nazi medallion round his neck which Mr Ross presumed was sported as an indication of masculinity and power. On the other hand, Alf surprised him one afternoon by spending a long time looking into the window of a model-shop and wishing he could afford some of the big ship-construction kits. Mr Ross comments, 'He is not past enjoyment of such things, despite his worldly ways.' He tends to assume that Alf's concern to assert his masculinity in the way of his peer culture precludes him from the normal, less threatening interests of any boy of his age. Only over the course of time does he really appreciate Alf's relative immaturity. In March, when he is not yet fifteen, the boy is having to look for some permanent job and Mr Ross only now realizes how unready he is for such a responsibility.

Had I realized earlier what Alf was up against, in himself and in his environment, I would have helped him apply for jobs through the usual channels.

This comment came after a long discussion between Mr Ross and the boy, whom he had tried to persuade to apply for jobs advertised in the local paper. To his consternation Alf scorned this idea, since in his opinion any job advertised in this way would automatically be above him. He thought that even labouring jobs that were advertised would require some paper qualification to warrant the advertisement. He appeared to think that he was precluded from applying. On further reflection Mr Ross was forced to the conclusion that lack of confidence was only part of the story:

I suspect his ability to read the appointments column with any degree of comprehension . . . even if he had selected some jobs to apply for I am sure he would have no idea of how to write a letter of application, even if he is capable of the actual mechanical activity of producing comprehensible writing – which I sometimes doubt.

I asked if he had contacted the youth employment officer or careers master. Alf said he had seen both but they were no good. Whether this meant that they were not interested in him or whether the procedure was again beyond him I am not sure. I suspect the latter, since he admitted that when he was supposed to visit the youth employment officer the second time he skipped school and went home.

The end of the term was only a week away and with almost everyone else in the class with a job to go to Mr Ross began more and more to share Alf's anxieties about his future. He eventually agreed to drive Alf to the factory where Harold had got his job to see if they would take him as well. Mr Ross was forced to explain the situation to the girl at the reception desk as Alf was so acutely nervous by the time they arrived that he seemed incapable of acting on his own. The personnel officer agreed to interview the boy and, having invited Mr Ross to accompany him, placed him behind Alf in a 'smutty room' at the back of the factory.

Although Mr Ross had thoughtfully talked to Alf about the sorts of questions he might be asked during the interview, he was totally unprepared for Alf's inarticulateness in response to the most simple questions asked by the personnel officer. Mr Ross made notes during the interview and the dialogue which follows represents the gist of what was said:

INTERVIEWER: What is your name?
ALF: Alf W. . . .
INT.: Alf what?
ALF: Waddy.
INT.: W-A-D-D-Y?
ALF: Yes.
INT.: Any other name?
ALF: No.
INT.: Address?
ALF: 7 Hillside Close.
INT.: Where is that?

ALF: Hillview.

INT.: Hillview. What's your father's name?

ALF: Mr Waddy.

INT.: Yes, but what's his Christian name?

ALF: I dunno.

INT.: You don't know?

ALF: No.

INT.: You don't know your father's name?

ALF: No ...

INT.: What does your mother call him?

ALF: Dunno ... er er oh yes, I think it's Trevor.

INT.: Trevor Waddy?

ALF: I think so.

INT.: Where does he work?

ALF: What's it, er um, what's it um, Paddington.

INT.: Paddington in London?

ALF: No, um what's it called?

INT.: You mean the railway station here?

ALF: Yeah, that's it, the railway.

INT.: What does he do?

ALF: Um ... um ... a driver.

INT.: Lorry driver?

ALF: No.

INT.: What then?

ALF: Train driver.

INT.: What school are you at?

ALF: Hillview.

INT.: Which form are you in?

ALF: Fourth.

INT.: Four what?

ALF: Dunno.

INT.: Well, is it four 'a' or 'b' or what?

ALF: Oh, four 'h'.

INT.: Does the four 'h' mean that it's a low stream in the fourth year?

ALF: I dunno.

INT.: What are your best subjects at school?

ALF: ...

INT.: Which do you enjoy most?

ALF: Well – games – gardening – maths – pottery.

INT.: Do you do woodwork?
ALF: Yes.
INT.: But it is not one of your favourites?
ALF: No.
INT.: Yet you are applying to work in a furniture factory?
ALF: ...
INT.: Do you read books much?
ALF: Not really.
INT.: How about the papers?
ALF: Yes, I read that sometimes.
INT.: Which paper do you read?
ALF: Dad's.
INT.: What's that?
ALF: Dunno.
INT.: The *Gazette* perhaps?
ALF: Yes, that's it.
INT.: Do you read it every day?
ALF: No.
INT.: Why not?
ALF: Well my reading is not too good.
INT.: How good? ... Can you read this?
ALF: (*stumbles after a few words.*)
INT.: Mmm.

Sharing this ordeal with Alf provided Mr Ross with an abrupt and shocking confirmation of his previous conjectures about the boy's capabilities. He suspected that Alf was not so much ignorant of his father's Christian name, but simply lacking in the knowledge of what was meant by the term 'Christian name'. Only Mr Ross knew that Alf's apparent ignorance of his father's occupation probably masked the fact that Mr Waddy was either unemployed or in prison. Although the boy had always assiduously avoided talking about his father to Mr Ross, he had learnt some of the facts about him from the Hillview youth-club leader. Alf had been sufficiently stirred by the questions about his father to make up a story about him for the interviewer, but he was quite unable to cover up his own deficiencies. Moreover, the physical environment of the interview, a dirty, shabby room, and the purpose of the confrontation, to find out if Alf was suited to a labouring job without any apprenticeship or training, underlined for Mr Ross the hopelessness of Alf's situation and the poor outlook for his future. After his failure to get work in this particular factory, where he would have been with his mate Harold, Alf got a job for himself a few days later. This did little to alleviate Mr Ross's disappointment, for the job was merely shifting timber and sweeping up, for a wage of £5 a week after stoppages.

Mr Ross's relationship with Alf throughout the year was marked largely by feelings of disappointment or frustration. Yet through the relationship he gained some insight into the lack of confidence which lay at the root of Alf's 'apathy'. He learnt too – and was shocked by – the appalling lack of preparedness with which many of our fifteen-year-olds leave school to enter upon adult responsibilities.

For many children the last year at school is a time of crisis. This is borne out by delinquency statistics, which tend to rise during the year before leaving school. There were certainly children involved in the project who followed this pattern. Several were put on probation, two were placed in remand homes, and more were certainly engaged in illegal activities of various sorts which went undetected. In their relationships with the children outside the school situation, the students were able to place behaviour of this kind in the context of the whole personality of the child. The boys who had not withdrawn completely tended to act out their feelings of frustration and rejection by truancy and acts of petty theft and destruction, while the girls in their search for adult roles tended to express their dissatisfactions through precocious sexual experience.

One example of this was Tess, who was described by her student after one of the first meetings with her as displaying no interest in what they were doing on Wednesday afternoons.

She looked straight ahead, eyes expressionless behind her glasses. When I asked her a question she answered abruptly, almost inaudibly, avoiding my eyes. Her attitude towards everything seemed negative or half-hearted.

Miss Spillsbury, the student, had however managed to find out a certain amount about Tess, who thought that school was terrible and looked forward to leaving it. She did not want to do anything in particular when she left, but would probably work in a local factory where some of her friends were employed. She spoke a little about her home and her two brothers, one younger and one older than herself, both of whom she said she disliked. With her pocket money of ten shillings a week she bought records and fabric to make herself clothes. As a child she had attended several junior schools, but she did not say why she had had to move. Miss Spillsbury's general impression was of a shy girl who rarely volunteered any information in an animated way, and who would only answer questions as though she were being interviewed. Her withdrawal and silence in social situations were further evidence to Miss Spillsbury of the girl's extreme lack of confidence and shyness. In a restaurant in the Students' Union she became very giggly and nervous and her hands shook as she sat at the table.

As time went on, though Tess continued to act in the same way with Miss Spillsbury, she noticed that the rest of the class, whom they sometimes came across on Wednesday afternoons, seemed frequently to regard her as something of a nonconformist. Then, through conversation with the class teacher, Miss Spillsbury learnt about the difficulties of Tess's home life. Her mother had lost all control over her, and her father, who had been a cripple, had died some years previously. Her mother had remarried and there was a mutual antipathy between Tess and her stepfather. The parents were constantly under the threat of prosecution for Tess's bad school attendance. It appeared that she was often out until two or three in the morning, and her mother had found it impossible to see that she went to school. The class teacher was convinced that she was sexually promiscuous.

Eventually, on one occasion when Miss Spillsbury was able to take Tess out on her own, she came closer to the girl, who by this time had learnt to trust her. They had intended to visit a discotheque, but when they found it closed Tess herself suggested they should walk round some department stores. Miss Spillsbury was both relieved and pleased to discover how comparatively relaxed a companion Tess could be. She talked much more openly about herself:

Her life seems pretty rough. She was limping because she had hurt her foot in a fight with her brother. Talking about the gang she went around with, it was clear that she was always the one who got hit. There are four girls and about twenty-six boys in the gang. They seem pretty destructive. I pointed to a skirt with felt flowers appliqued on to the hem, saying I liked it, and she said, 'Ha, they'd soon get pulled off!'

The gang does not take her right away from her home as I imagined. She told me they often came to her house and waited outside for her. If it was raining they'd come in and play cards. The evening usually ended in a row with her mother as she tried to get them to go home. They never took any notice of her, said Tess.

Miss Spillsbury began to learn more about Tess, not so much about the things she did, but rather about the things that happened to her, particularly the unpleasant things. Like Alf she semed to have little capacity for enjoyment – partly perhaps because few enjoyable experiences came her way. She seemed to take pleasure in doing some printing in the art studio, but all she could say about it was that it was 'nice'. Even then her interest quickly flagged and she had washed her hands and was ready to leave quite some time before the others. Miss Spillsbury remarks at this time, when she had known Tess for about a month, that most of her knowledge about the girl's difficulties had come from the class teacher and the head. When she was with Miss Spillsbury Tess behaved quietly, too quietly in fact, participating as little as possible in any group activity, and displaying positive individuality only by conspicuously wearing her own clothes while the others in the group were wearing school uniforms. Even at this stage there is a sharp contrast between the way Miss Spillsbury sees Tess and the notorious reputation she has at school among teachers and classmates.

About a month later Tess invited the student and another girl to her home to meet her mother, and Miss Spillsbury was able to learn at first hand something of the difficulties of Tess's home life. In next to no time Tess's mother had told the visitors all about her first husband, Tess's father, who had had an accident which had paralysed him when Tess was small, and had died some years later. Tess was understandably upset and embarrassed at her mother's revelations. The experience of her father's death seemed to be still a painful reality with which both mother and daughter were trying to cope. Yet they appeared not to have joined forces to support one another; rather, there was a good deal of tension between them. On this particular occasion Tess rudely tried to shut her mother up, while the mother appealed to Miss Spillsbury to witness the bad behaviour of her daughter.

After Christmas Tess asked Miss Spillsbury to her home again and on the way there described how her mother had had a drink and a good talk with an older sister that morning and was a lot more cheerful than she had been for some time. Tess's mother was at home and they had tea and talked. Miss Spillsbury was able to see Tess's position more clearly:

The mother is uncertain of people, anxious to please, and looks tired and hardworked. She can't find it very easy to give Tess help when she has her own problems. Tess seems to have given up action of any sort, except what will shock her mother and force her to give her attention (e.g. boys, late nights, drink, smoking). Her apathy is more than the usual adolescent apathy and her behaviour is more extreme than the difficult behaviour commonly associated with adolescents.

Miss Spillsbury describes Tess as a miserable and helpless member of a whole family characterized by lack of initiative: her stepfather seemed to be largely ignored by her mother; the mother was shy and lonely on the estate where they lived, knowing none of the neighbours. She was full of good resolutions about planning her life more successfully, which she confessed she never had time to carry out. Tess herself had never discussed the exact nature of her own relationship and experience with men, but Miss Spillsbury was convinced by this

time that at fourteen she was behaving in an unusually promiscuous way. She felt that part of the explanation for such
behaviour might have been the lack of stability at home which
she had herself witnessed. Any promiscuity seemed 'more a sign
of maladjustment than that of an experienced woman of the
world'. After this meeting Tess absented herself from school
and did not meet Miss Spillsbury until four weeks later, when
she anounced that she would probably be leaving Hillview to
go to another school for training. Miss Spillsbury guessed that
she was in some sort of trouble, but did not like to go on asking
questions as the girl was being deliberately vague. It was on the
following Wednesday afternoon that Miss Spillsbury, calling at
the school to collect Tess, discovered from a classmate that the
girl was pregnant. The class teacher, who was very upset, had
been told that there was no need to take any steps over Tess's
bad attendance in future. She was to be marked absent on the
class register, but as far as the school was concerned it seemed
she was no longer their responsibility. The class teacher had
not been given any information about Tess's pregnancy. Miss
Spillsbury's comments on that afternoon are important because
they underline what we have tried to say about the way children
are looked at in schools and how, inevitably it seems, their
problems tend to become compartmentalized:

The thing that appalled me most of all was the lack of communication between all the people who had something to do with Tess.
There seemed to be no common fund of information about her
case. The welfare officer knew a bit, the class teacher knew a bit, the
mother had lost control. Who is responsible for the poor kid?

Miss Spillsbury, encouraged by the class teacher and the discussion in the tutorial group, decided that it was important to
keep in touch with Tess as she might need someone to talk to.
She did so, though the girl did not find it by any means easy to
talk about her situation. In fact she avoided discussing the
matter in every way she could, first by bringing her small
brother along on outings and then by pretending to be out

when Miss Spillsbury in desperation called at her home. After this occasion Miss Spillsbury made the difficult decision to write and ask Tess why she had not opened the door and why she had run away. She explained that she had heard that Tess was expecting a baby and expressed the hope that this would not make any difference to their meetings. When she visited Tess's house again the door was opened by the elder brother, who said she had gone to the mother-and-baby home that afternoon but she had left a note. Tess's letter gave the address and telephone number of the home. Miss Spillsbury writes, 'I was terribly pleased and felt almost like crying.'

At the home for unmarried mothers Miss Spillsbury was able to talk to Tess in her dormitory, a large and impersonal place like a hospital ward. It seemed that Tess was going to be terribly lonely, as her mother, because she worked during the week and had the two boys to look after, could only visit her on Saturday afternoons. Besides her loneliness there was the problem of boredom. The girls were apparently allowed out only in the mornings after doing an hour's housework. Tess then had nothing to do except to look forward to the evenings when there was television to watch. She also had to try to cope with the fact that her baby would be adopted and as a consequence she would not be allowed to take any interest in it. When Miss Spillsbury suggested that the baby might need something to wear, whatever happened to it, Tess said resentfully, that of course they would not put it into her clothes, they would dress it up in something posh when it went to be adopted. It was not surprising that Tess's feelings were very confused; still only fourteen, she was in the midst of a situation which would be distressing even to an older woman. However, as time went on, she was able to speak more freely to Miss Spillsbury and describe her embarrassment and nervousness about being seen in public – she was very large by then. Her questions to Miss Spillsbury about what she was doing with the other girls in the class revealed a wistful longing, tinged perhaps with bitterness, to be back with them, just to be an ordinary schoolgirl. She was not going to admit it openly however: 'I wonder if they all miss me up there – I don't miss them at all.' It was with the same bravado that she said she did not care about the baby. One day she was playing fondly with the baby of another girl at the home, who teased her by saying, 'Tess won't be able to leave hers!' Tess quickly told her that she could have it as a gift any time.

Miss Spillbury's journal ends here – she finished the course and left and we have no further knowledge of Tess. It is quite clear, however, that Miss Spillsbury got to know Tess more fully than most of the other adults that surrounded her, and perhaps more closely than the friends of her own age. She was able to establish a good relationship with her, non-authoritarian but concerned, and had the time to seek her out despite all obstacles. As a consequence she managed to gain the confidence of Tess, who was enabled to break through the rebellious attitude she had towards most adults in authority. At the same time, though Miss Spillsbury was a friend, she was also an adult and so Tess had less need to keep up appearances than she had with her peer group.

The case of another girl, Brenda, throws further light on the little understood area of the sexual behaviour of girls at school. Miss Turpin writing in her journal shows her appreciation of a child who, unlike the others we have mentioned, is not marked by apparent apathy but on the contrary has a positive enjoyment of life. Brenda, a brassy blonde, dashed home from school every Wednesday dinner hour to change into her miniskirt and high heels, assuring Miss Turpin that she 'wouldn't be seen dead walking round town in school uniform'. She took a delight in rummaging around antique shops in town. She enjoyed walking on a misty, blustery day despite brief showers of rain. At the swimming pool she forced herself to swim a width in order to gain the approbation of two of the boys in her class – she told Miss Turpin later she had not realized before that they were quite so dishy. She impressed Miss Turpin with the quality of her imagination as she looked at paintings and sculptures in the art gallery, and with her readiness to offer her opinions and interpretations. At the same time she hated school and described most of the teachers as 'horrible'. Miss Turpin felt that her attitude to authority was strongly influenced by her relationship with her father, whom she seemed to regard as a rather harsh tyrant. Brenda's home conditions were poor and overcrowded. It became increasingly plain that she felt she got little sympathy, support or guidance from either of her parents.

Miss Turpin enjoyed the outings with Brenda on Wednesday afternoons and missed her 'infectious hilarity' when Brenda's truancy left her alone with the other, rather shy, member of the group. She was in her element at the Christmas party, being the most practised dancer in the class, and she greatly enjoyed displaying her skill. She was highly flattered when one of the men students danced with her and in the brief intervals, when she collapsed on her chair, she kept saying, 'He's a good un, Ronnie, ain't he?' Despite her enjoyment of life there were subtleties in Brenda's personality which only gradually revealed themselves to Miss Turpin. For the first two weeks of the spring term, instead of coming to the Wednesday meetings, she apparently spent the afternoon with her boyfriend Mike. Miss Turpin went with the other girl in her group to visit Brenda and to ask her what her feelings were about their outings together. In fact, she asked Brenda if she were fed up with them:

We needn't have worried. Brenda shrieked with delight when she saw us. 'Ere Mike, look who has come to see us!' She took us into the front room where she and Mike had been keeping each other warm – it was very cold. Brenda was laughing and talking her head off as usual. She seemed most surprised that I should think she might be fed up – denied it most emphatically and was quite touched at my concern.

Miss Turpin found it difficult to reconcile Brenda's apparent enthusiasm for the outings on Wednesdays and her eager participation in their activities with this absenteeism and lack of staying power. She felt that Brenda's real feelings were very hard to gauge and that her bright exterior, broken by occasional flashes of temper, might well be a mask for a troubled inner life. Despite her physical maturity she lacked the ability to sustain any lasting relationship with her boyfriend. After he had heard stories about her sleeping around and had refused to speak to her in public, Brenda's response was simply to walk away, shouting abuse as she went. There was a childlike side to Brenda's character which emerges from Miss Turpin's description of a visit to a dog's home. Brenda survived a long bus ride and a wearisome trek on foot to the home where she rushed from cage to cage in delight; ignoring the overpowering stench, she was prevented with difficulty from acquiring a dog, and consoled herself instead with nine guinea pigs. She nonchalantly disregarded the curious looks of passers-by at the box which she carried and from which issued dreadful squealings and drops of blood.

On the bus a rather refined lady with a very refined accent inquired what we had in the box and then why we wanted so many guinea pigs. Brenda snapped back, 'To breed them, of course!'

During that very same afternoon Miss Turpin learnt more of the contrasting elements in Brenda's life. Her love-affair with Mike appeared to have been irrevocably broken, and although she was still very fond of him she had someone else. She appeared embarrassed to the point of shame over her physical involvement with a boy she did not really care about. It seemed to Miss Turpin that the only constant element in Brenda's diverse behaviour was her need for love and affection: whether the answer was to be found in boyfriends or pets depended on the swing of her adolescent emotions. By her classmates and the other adults who knew her Brenda was merely dismissed as promiscuous, but Miss Turpin, through her increasing insight, was able to view the girl with good-humoured sympathy. This emerges during a visit to the zoo:

Brenda was in her element – talked learnedly about various animals – strained over the railings to put her hand in the cages of lion cubs! – and proudly guided me round the zoo whose layout she knows by heart. The highlight of her afternoon was the sight of two rhinos copulating in the middle of their yard. She stood gazing in great fascination for over twenty minutes, occasionally murmuring under her breath in an awed undertone, 'Cor – 'e's a dirty bugger – just look at the filthy sod!' She was full of sympathy for the female rhino, whose sides were covered in blood where the hoofs of her excited partner had rubbed up and down!

In May Brenda confided to Miss Turpin that she and the new boyfriend, Gordon, were contemplating marriage:

As we walked down the main street she brought me up to date on the present state of her love life. If she is still going out with Gordon at Christmas then they are going to get engaged (he is fifteen – she is fourteen). I commented that this was rather a sudden turn of events – I thought she wasn't very keen on him before. She said she wasn't sure whether she liked him for the sake of liking him or whether she liked him for himself. Also she thought they would probably break up long before Christmas, but if they hadn't, then she might as well marry him. I said she'd better make sure that she did not *have* to get married before then. . . . Later on she described the proposal scene in detail. She said she was sitting on the sofa larking about as usual when suddenly Gordon 'goes all serious' – he drew her up to him and said, 'Brenda, I loves you.' At this point Brenda, partly from embarrassment, partly from surprise, had difficulty in suppressing her laughter, but managed to say, 'I didn't think to hear that from you, Gordon.'

Miss Turpin is able to act as confidante rather than moralist partly because she sees Brenda in the context of her family life as well as her sex life. Her visits to Brenda's home as well as conversations with her over a long period had revealed very difficult living conditions. Brenda's family lived in a three-bedroomed house; she and her two younger sisters shared one room; her sister, newly back from New Zealand, shared another with her husband and baby, while the third bedroom had been turned into a sitting-room for them. Brenda's parents slept in the living room while the kitchen was used as a cooking-dining-sitting-room. The situation was further complicated by the fact that Brenda's sister was expecting another baby and was very moody and depressed, having had her name down on a list for a council house for some months without success. Brenda seemed very fond of her sister, expressed understanding of her moods, and hoped for her sake that she would get a place for her family soon. Apparently, although Brenda had difficulties of her own, she was sympathetic to the problems of others:

She has a very warm, sympathetic character and is mature for her age – more mature in fact than most girls who leave school at eighteen. Certainly I see no reason for calling her educationally deprived. She has a vitality and spontaneity that would be envied by lots of people.

It is not easy even for Miss Turpin to sort out the complexities of Brenda's personality and situation. She understands the pressures that arise from the discomfort and the lack of privacy in her home and is struck by the warmth of her feelings for other people. Yet there is evidence too that Brenda is in some ways far from mature – is still in need of guidance through her adolescence.

Later in the year Miss Turpin became increasingly worried by rumours she heard from students and children involved in the project that Brenda might be pregnant, and she began to try to help Brenda to talk. Miss Turpin's frankness about her own views on sex enabled Brenda to talk openly about her various affairs. She had always refused to take precautions, and in the case of Gordon had actually torn off a sheath the first time he had tried to use one. The fears of becoming pregnant seemed at first largely concerned with her parents' reactions. Her father had repeatedly warned her not to bring any trouble home, and only a few nights before Miss Turpin's discussion with her they had had a violent quarrel after she had come home late. Her father had hit her and called her a dirty cow, and Brenda had lost her temper and hit him back, calling him a 'fucking-faced bastard'. At this point all hell was let loose and Brenda had finally run out saying she wasn't going to come back. Apparently she had done this before and her parents had asked the police to search for her. She told Miss Turpin that they had since used this incident as a threat, and had told her that as she was out of their control the police would take her and put her in a home at the least hint of trouble. Not unnaturally Brenda was terrified of this possibility. As she talked it became obvious that she and Gordon had often discussed the real possibility of a baby and that Gordon had promised to stand by her, although they both feared the anger of Brenda's parents. There was no doubt that the girl had for a long time needed to confide in an adult she could trust. All the way back to Miss Turpin's flat she clung to her arm in relief and gratitude. At last Brenda admitted that she had missed a period and was worried that she might be actually pregnant. She agreed to see a doctor for an examination and pregnancy test on the understanding that Miss Turpin would come with her and would also support her if she had to tell her parents the worst. The worst, as it turned out, might well have been that she could not identify the probable father, for as well as Gordon she had had intercourse with three other boys, one of whom was the leader of a local gang. This meant that she could be in serious trouble with the authorities as her parents had threatened; and if Gordon found out about her other affairs he might abandon her. Furthermore, if he did accept the responsibility for fatherhood he could be charged with the offence of having intercourse with a girl under the age of sixteen. As if this were not complicated enough, it seemed clear that Brenda may in some sense have wanted to have a baby – partly to have something of her own to love, partly perhaps to pay her parents back for their lack of trust and sympathy. Fortunately, on this occasion, the alarm was a false one: the visit to the doctor proved that Brenda was not pregnant. Miss Turpin's relief, as well as Brenda's, can be imagined. Through sharing, as a friend, in Brenda's distress she had come to understand the complexities and human contradictions which lay beneath the surface of an apparently easy-going and self-sufficient girl.

Shirley, Alf, Harold, Tess and Brenda have been chosen for discussion in this chapter either because they are particularly well described in student journals or because they stand out as personalities in their own right. It would obviously be unwise

from the nature of our evidence to generalize too readily about
characteristics of personality or behaviour. One generalization
we wish to make though is that schools and teacher-training
institutions as they are today give the teacher a very partial
knowledge of many, if not all, of the children he encounters.
There is surely a strong case for ensuring that all teachers in
training have some experience of getting to know at least a few
children in depth.

Chapter 4
Authority and the Young Teacher

In the next three chapters we propose to look more closely at some specific areas in which young teachers are likely to find difficulty in coming to terms with reluctant learners. The first area, and the one which most exercises the young or intending teacher, is his ability to control the children he teaches. The anxiety which every teacher initially feels as he faces the prospect of meeting large groups of children who may not share his interests or concern for learning cannot be overestimated. If he is to deal with his anxiety in a rational and effective way he needs some understanding both of the complexity of the nature of authority itself and of his own basic attitudes towards it.

The Hillview project places the student in a position of responsibility towards the children in his group outside the institutional structure of the school. As a result of this, conflicts that inevitably arise between students and children have to be resolved without recourse to traditional sanctions. This is clearly not an exact parallel with the normal classroom situation, but, because the student is in a position where he has to define both his role and his task, we believe the project is particularly productive of student learning. On many occasions students have been faced with challenges to their authority which forced them to examine the nature of their responsibility. They could not fall back on automatic responses sanctioned by tradition. They used journals and tutorial sessions to present and to begin to sort out the complexities of the exercise of authority in a variety of situations. On one occasion one of the students, Mr Andrews, told us about his attempts to interest two boys in doing some painting. They showed little interest, partly because they had originally wanted to spend the afternoon in some local woods where they could practise with the air-pistols they were still carying hidden beneath their jackets.

The afternoon was an unsuccessful one, but at the end of it the student invited the boys back to his flat for tea. On the way one of them began firing his pistol in the street and Mr Andrews tried to stop him. He told us that he said to the boy in a mild tone 'I'd rather you didn't do that', trying not to aggravate the sullenness which had been building up during the afternoon. A second request in the same pleasant tone and phrased in the same unassuming manner was also ignored. In the group tutorial discussion afterwards Mr Andrews said, 'They came back to my flat and shot off their guns into the street. I didn't know what attitude to take; I asked them not to shoot into the street and they took no notice.' He felt very strongly that he wanted to avoid an out-and-out confrontation with the boys – he was particularly concerned about the more aggressive of them, fearing the influence he might have on the others later.

Mr Andrews was in a dilemma here: his main concern at this stage was to maintain a good and friendly relationship with both boys, yet he could not ignore such an incident. Clearly the proper thing for any responsible adult to do in this situation was to insist that the boys put the pistols away. Even in discussion, though, Mr Andrews seemed reluctant to acknowledge this. It was as though his fear of endangering the relationship and his uncertainty about the nature of his authority over the boys was preventing him from acting in a spontaneously responsible way. In the classroom the choice would be more simple: few experienced teachers would have any qualms about confiscating air-pistols should they appear. The teacher knows that action of this kind would have the support of everyone, his colleagues, his head and, if it came to it, the local authority. Had the incident occurred in the classroom Mr Andrews might well have behaved in a similar way. Nevertheless, young teachers cannot be as certain of their authority as older teachers and may often find themselves unable to act decisively in situations where decision is called for. This particular response – the half-hearted attempt to gain cooperation from children who are behaving badly – was typical of more than one of the students who took part in the project, and is a common one for the student teacher and for young teachers in general. The problem is made more acute perhaps by the prevailing climate of opinion in many colleges and departments of education. Students sometimes see recommendations to liberal and progressive approaches, quite wrongly of course, as an inducement to abdicate from all exercise of authority. Many teachers will remember early experiences with difficult classes where they found themselves repeating feeble injunctions to keep quiet which were just ignored. One of us was supervising a student on teaching practice in just such a situation. She was surprised to be advised to act more firmly, though the reason she could not carry out the lesson was chiefly, it seemed, because she was afraid to risk the children's displeasure. Her response to the advice was, 'Oh, I didn't think you approved of us being strict!' There was no justification for such a belief, yet this kind of fantasy is not uncommon: it is almost as if student teachers wilfully misunderstand what is presented on education courses. The education staff in general are used as justification for the student's own inability to be responsible for what happens in his classroom. It must be said too that sometimes teachers in schools aid and abet this kind of interpretation. It is of course understandable that the young teacher, uncertain of himself as a person of authority, should try to protect himself in such a way. The anxiety the new teacher feels in the classroom, faced by a group of adolescents whose behaviour is unpredictable and potentially hostile, inevitably reduces his capacity to perceive clearly and to judge objectively, and it is not unusual to find student teachers operating in the classroom well below their capacity outside it. We have already suggested that this kind of anxiety may be reduced if the student during his period of training can be helped to explore in a sympathetic environment his experience of authority and his feelings about it. Only then can he begin to work out adequate ways of exercising authority himself.

Students on the Hillview project were sometimes pushed into extreme situations through their reluctance to act authoritatively. Mr Dash had taken two boys for the weekend to a friend's cottage and this is the account of the occasion he wrote in his journal:

Reg, Mike and I arrived at the cottage early; there was an air-gun there which the landlady had said they could use if they brought their own pellets, so of course they couldn't wait to get their hands on it! One thing she had stipulated about its use however was that it should not be used on her goldfish. I forgot to remind them about this, and within an hour the goldfish was mortally wounded. Mike's comment was that he was only trying to make it move, which I thought was true as far as conscious reasons go. But on another level it was just another example of the incredibly compulsive and irrational way they behave sometimes; I suppose whatever warning I could have given them it would still have happened and they would have still felt compelled to do something which would endanger the goldfish! The next day, after this crisis was over, the gun was handed out again and the boys disappeared to shoot birds. The number of birds within shooting range however was limited, and the target soon became Reg, who came rushing into the house to the sound of pinging pellets. Mike came into the house shortly after-wards and started twisting Reg's arm, which made him cry. What had caused these incidents? If I had hung around while they used the gun I suppose they would have behaved more sensibly, but not of their own accord. On both occasions I talked with them about what they had done. . . . Over the goldfish I was as philosophical as possible and pointed out that I was as embarrassed and ashamed as they were (I thought it pointless to add that killing was senseless because they could see that anyway); over the second incident all I could think of to say to Mike was that I didn't chase him with a gun just because I was stronger than him. No comment!

Mr Dash was an intelligent and thoughtful man, outgoing, friendly and positive. He was involved enough with the project to give up a weekend in order to take the boys into the country. He wanted to keep the occasion an informal one and so avoided any kind of preliminary discussions with the boys about how they should behave in the cottage. In his comment on his for-getting to warn them about the goldfish he expresses the opinion that, considering 'the compulsive and irrational' behaviour of the boys, something extreme would have happened whatever he had said or done. After the goldfish incident he did talk to them and obviously gave some thought to the most useful and constructive things to say, trying to relate his own and the boys' experience in a way that would be meaningful to them. However, what he said seems to have had little effect and the bullying incident follows. Mr Dash clearly knew that Mike was in the habit of victimizing the other boy, but seems not to have been able to use the opportunity offered by the weekend together to try to sort out the sources of the friction. He once again avoided real discussion of the boys' behaviour and his last words 'No comment!' seems to suggest his own dissatisfaction with what he was able to achieve. Perhaps the most crucial sentence in his account is 'If I had hung around while they used the gun I suppose they would have behaved more sensibly, but not of their own accord.' It is as if he saw all intervention on his part as authoritarian, and for that reason invalid. If the boys could not behave well when left to themselves he was certainly not going to make them do otherwise. He sees no difference between the kind of support that an adult can give while children are working through gradual stages in their acceptance of responsibility, and the kind of adult behaviour which lays out all the rules from the top down.

It may be that Mr Dash had not yet resolved the conflict created by his own childhood experience of authority. It seemed that part of him wished to reject authority of any kind and yet, as he showed on other occasions, part of him had taken over without reflection the pattern of authority he had experienced. We have the impression that quite a few young teachers attracted to working with the more rebellious kind of child are in a similar position. However much they may have coped with their own problems of authority in their growth towards adulthood, when they are placed in a position of authority over children, they tend to suffer a reactivation of old conflicts. For instance, some men in particular who have been at odds with their fathers may have such vivid recollections of their own stress that they cannot bear the risk of a similar relationship with the children they have charge of. They need to be helped to gain sufficient insight into their attitudes to this kind of situation to be purposeful and directive when the need arises. As outsiders to the actual events in all such cases, we cannot prescribe what the student should do, but we believe that an understanding by him of the motives for his behaviour can reduce anxiety and enable him to act constructively.

The kind of student we have described, uncertain of his leadership role, desiring to be friendly, relatively ineffectual in situations demanding firmness, will tend to arouse a certain kind of response from the children. They may at first welcome the friendliness, since it appears to allow them to be themselves. However they have certain expectations about the behaviour of the teacher or adult placed in charge of them. They expect him to want something of them and to set up before them clear standards of behaviour. It is as though there is a contract to teach and to be taught, to lead and to be led. In the beginning of any relationship there is an element of testing out the limits, as any experienced teacher knows very well. The kind of children we are concerned with are likely to expect, though they may not wish, those with authority to exert it in an inflexible way. Parents tend to be authoritarian rather than permissive; park keepers, bus conductors and shop assistants often regard them with suspicion rather than acceptance; their regular teachers will often have demanded from them obedience rather than cooperation. When approached by the young teacher with offers of friendly relations it is not surprising that they will want to test the nature and limits of such an offer. Where their first probe meets no obstacle the children may go further and further in their attempts to challenge the teacher's authority. Our examples show how dangerous and destructive these probes can become. It is often assumed that this kind of behaviour is evidence of devil-may-care toughness, but there is likely to be a great deal of anxiety for the children in such a situation. When their expectations about the teacher's behaviour are not met they easily become confused about what is expected of them. More than most, children of less than average ability tend to react negatively to new situations or unaccustomed demands. They will not always be hostile: they may become apathetic or indifferently polite. Many a young teacher who has offered a choice of new and interesting things to do knows the disconcerting shrug of the shoulders or the muttered 'I don't mind' which undermine all his efforts. The teacher who wishes to establish new patterns of behaviour and relationships in the classroom will not have an easy time. He will have to convince the class of his competence before they will readily forgo attitudes that have become familiar to them.

In order to avoid the risk of rejection a young teacher may attempt to sidestep any conflict by a kind of collusion with his pupils. A stereotyped view of such collusion is sometimes operated by the formal teacher, who describes his young colleague as 'currying favour with the children'. He may see this as a threat to the authority of the school and his own status, but in fact the reality of the situation is likely to be more complex. The young teacher, sympathetic to the children, may be tempted to join their ranks not so much to gain popularity but rather to avoid the burden of authority. At an early stage he may well feel isolated from the staff group and unable to identify with their aims. He may see them as formidably competent and feel himself very much the new boy of the school, so much so that he may be reluctant to go to them for help, and so may increase his own sense of isolation. In such a situation the children may seem a natural ally and he may be drawn to them to the extent of finding it impossible to teach effectively in the classroom. He will be tempted into a self-indulgent kind of informality, rising to the bait of whatever witticism the class offers, allowing himself to be distracted by any comments or suggestions, whether or not they contribute to the purpose of the lesson.

When a class senses that the teacher is uncertain of his role and of the boundaries which define it they will often further exploit this weakness, for instance, by asking intrusive questions about his personal life. We are often asked by student teachers how they should respond to questions about their sex life.

Initially such questions may be asked out of simple curiosity, but if the children sense any uncertainty in the response they can quickly become offensive and embarrassing. Equally, similar questions may be asked about other teachers. To the children this may seem an opportunity for splitting off the teacher from his colleagues. As in all such situations, if children succeed in the manoeuvre they are likely to be made even more anxious and confused by the realization of the power they have. The young teacher for his part may be tempted to accept information about his colleagues, because it seems an easy way of gaining support in a difficult situation. However, while he will probably feel some guilt at the implied betrayal of colleagues, he may be unaware of the further damage done to a deteriorating relationship with the class.

This kind of testing of the teacher's loyalty is a common feature in any classroom where a basically friendly relationship exists between teacher and pupils. Sometimes the teacher may be invited to collude with a child in making a choice which is morally wrong. For instance, one of us remembers a girl who confessed to her class teacher that she had told a series of lies to another teacher to avoid having to take part in the physical education lesson. She had often used the excuse that she was suffering from bad period pains, but the day came when she had cried wolf too often. On this occasion she really did have her period but could hardly expect to be believed since she had used the excuse to the PE mistress only a week before! Partly because of the difficult relationship between herself and the child, who was a powerful influence in the class, and partly because of her own antipathy to physical education, the class teacher found herself strongly tempted to keep in the child's good favour by suggesting another more plausible excuse. This kind of collusion between teacher and child easily leads to moral dilemmas for the teacher. One of our students involved in the Hillview project, Mr Quigley, describes himself in just such a predicament in a café with two boys:

Now all at once, I found myself in a difficult position, for the juke box was going wrong and, apart from playing the requested records, was disgorging sixpences and shillings at a fairly rapid rate. The boys were naturally delighted! As a result I found myself in the middle of a robbery of the juke box and my most advisable course of action was by no means clear. It *was* clear that the correct moral action would have set me well apart from them and detracted, to some extent, from the progress we had made during the past few weeks. I therefore took the 'Aren't we lucky!' approach, which must have sounded pretty lame but I was not keen to discourage them too actively. All this time of course I was desperately hoping that the flow of cash would cease, which it did quite soon. The boys then split the haul and returned to me the money for the snooker table and we went back to my flat.

Mr Quigley is quite clear that all this is wrong, but seems unable to do anything about it. He is not in the teacher's role here but nevertheless as a responsible adult feels that he cannot turn a blind eye to the situation. We might say that the child in him responds in the same way as the boys, 'Aren't we lucky!'; the adult in him just hopes that the machine will stop; and the parent in him knows that it is wrong to steal. Once again there is a fear of losing by an open confrontation the relationship that has been established. It seems to him that any discussion of the moral issues involved would inevitably seem censorious. His notion of authority is one that does not admit the possibility of consulting with the boys about the problem.

Mr Quigley is probably right in thinking that a straight condemnation of the boys' behaviour would, in the circumstances, have been useless. Just as much as his pretence that there was nothing wrong, an open condemnation would have made discussion of the theft impossible. Had he felt more sure of himself and of his relationship with the boys the incident could have been used constructively. If he could at least have shared with them his doubts about the morality of what they were doing, there would have been some possibility of fruitful learning. Teachers generally, perhaps because traditionally they have been seen as dispensers of moral truth, find it particularly difficult to discuss such issues in a genuinely open way. A teacher's free admission that he too in some situations is uncertain how he ought to act would free young people to engage meanfully in a genuine dialogue about what is right. Discussion of this kind, far from risking the rupture of good relationships, will do more than almost anything else to deepen them, as students often discover during the course of the project.

Although Mr Quigley was on this occasion unable to talk about the situation in the presence of the two boys, such experiences are often reflected upon later when the immediate stress is reduced. An extract from another student's journal both sharply raises the issue of the nature of adult responsibility in an informal relationship and also gives evidence of this particular student's growth of concern for the boys in his charge:

Another Wednesday the others came along with us for a walk in the woods. We decided to climb down into a gorge; having got to the bottom Jim wanted to climb a steep face of rock, and not wanting to seem chicken, Fred and I said we would too. After going about half way I lost my nerve and Fred was beginning to look pretty worried too. I turned back but Fred stuck it out and got to the top, which I have to admit raised my estimation of them considerably! The others had gone off in another direction so I hung around at the bottom feeling a bit ashamed of myself and worried stiff in case one of the boys fell (now I know what it feels like to be a responsible middle-class father!).

Anyway they made it to the top and I made my way the long way round. When I joined the others I found the other two boys had had to help Ian to get back up the easy way because he had got frightened and had started to cry. I think I should have stayed with Ian all the time because I think he felt that I had deserted him. Once again I think this brings home just how dependent he is.

Mr Vosper's difficulties in this hair-raising incident stemmed from the alacrity with which he took up the boys' challenge to climb the cliff. There is something engaging in this and in Mr Vosper's admiration for those who were successful. This kind of spontaneity in his relations with the young is one of the advantages the new teacher naturally possesses, and it is a quality that should be nurtured. If there is one thing that many secondary schools lack it is spontaneity, whether from pupils or their teachers. Too often the established teacher, seeing the possible dangers, becomes over-cautious and will not allow an exploratory situation to develop in the classroom. However, the impulsive behaviour of Mr Vosper, because he was unable to discuss freely with the boys his feelings about what they proposed, was clearly less than adequate. In essence this is the problem of the progressive young teacher in school: through his enthuiasm and feeling for children he is able to allow their spontaneity to emerge, yet he often has not acquired the professional skill to contain it and direct it into constructive channels. One of the aims of teacher education must be to hasten the process by which the young teacher acquires this skill.

The kind of reckless enterprise that Mr Vosper displayed on this occasion is by no means characteristic of all students in training. The educational experience of some will not have encouraged spontaneity or the wish to experiment. The relative security of teaching as a career does seem to attract some more cautious individuals. For them the challenge offered by children's lack of inhibition and by their inventiveness may be experienced as a threat. These very qualities imply a degree of unpredictability, and unpredictability is exactly what students of this kind are trying to avoid. When it does come their way they may deal with it by pretending that it does not exist. On teaching practice we have sometimes observed students, in noisy classrooms where children are behaving with little regard for them or for the purpose of the lesson, blandly carrying on as though all was well. This of course may be partly due to the strain of trying not to appear to be at a loss before their supervisors. It is difficult to help such students, though, when, even in discussion afterwards, they cannot acknowledge to themselves how unsatisfactory the situation really was. It is as though their concept of the orderly lesson was too powerful to admit of any modification by reality. Together with this view of the lesson as a carefully structured pattern is the tendency to treat the class as one entity. Any acknowledgement of individual diversity, whether it is constructive or disturbing, is seen

as a threat to the whole enterprise. Yet teaching which is satisfying to both children and teacher must include procedures
which make it possible to use individual contributions as they
arise. Means have to be found to help young teachers to cope
with their fears of the variety and unexpectedness of individual
response.

When a teacher is insufficiently flexible to deal with the
unexpected he will respond to the conflict this gives rise to in a
number of ways. One of them is effectively to abdicate from
all claim to authority. This degree of abdication is exceptional
in the classroom, but because of the relatively unstructured
nature of the Hillview project we came across a good many
examples of it. On one occasion Miss Lucas had arranged to
take her two boys back to her flat for the afternoon:

As we did not have much time that afternoon we went first to the
tower and planned to walk to the flat later. When I got to the tower
they had squeezed themselves in (through the turnstile without
paying) ... they were uncertain what to do – whether to behave
and do what I suggested or to disobey me deliberately. They decided on the latter, because they refused to come down the tower.
They were not unpleasant and were quite cheerful – they merely
sat at the top, smoking and talking, while I waited in good humour
down below. Eventually they came down and we started off down
the path. They had obviously decided, however, that they did not
want to come to the flat and began to walk slowly up another
path.

What seems to us significant here is not so much the boys'
behaviour or Miss Lucas's avoidance of confrontation with
them, but rather her self-deception and inability to admit to
herself that the situation was beyond her control. The phrase
'I waited in good humour' was surely a denial of the feelings of
anger and rejection which would have been entirely reasonable
at such a time. Indeed, Miss Lucas spoke rather more feelingly
in discussion afterwards. Perhaps, like so many young teachers,
she was unable to express her aggression openly at the time for
fear that she might be more destructive than she intended. She

was wise not to go up the tower and attempt to drag the boys down; on the other hand, if she had let them know that she was angry no harm would have been done and the relationship might have been strengthened. It was clearly important that the boys should realize that she too had feelings. A reluctance to disclose personal feelings before children is rather common among teachers. Indeed the suppression of feeling sometimes seems almost one of the undeclared aims of the secondary school, going far beyond the restraint normal in our society. The recognition that anger or hurt or concern can be openly expressed in the relationship between teacher and child is vital if such a relationship is to have any authenticity. The young teacher cannot be confident in his authority if he is unable to acknowledge, even to himself, his real feelings.

The suppression of feeling in schools sometimes leads to that exercise of authority known as 'clamping down'. We may define this as an inflexible and aggressive overruling by the teacher of anything that stands in the way of what he sees as his purpose in the lesson. Such behaviour by the teacher is invariably accompanied by threats and by punishment, and completely blocks any opportunity for initiative on the part of the class. In such a situation there can be no genuine dialogue between teacher and child. There is no evidence in student journals or in what we have learned from discussion to suggest that this happened more than once or twice on the Hillview project. No doubt this can be explained by the size of the groups, the relatively unrestricted circumstances under which they met, and the absence of a structured curriculum. It does suggest though that, whatever the strains, it was possible for the relationship between student and child to be maintained. The students' feelings were engaged, and the relationship, although not always agreeable, was firm enough, we think, to help them acquire some insight into their own attitudes to the exercise of adult authority.

Whatever happens during his teacher-training course, whatever insights he gains into the proper exercise of authority, much will still depend on the way the young teacher is received

in his first post. Too often he is persuaded by the staff of the
school into the belief that his chief function as teacher is to
keep good order. The young teacher on his very first visit to a
new school may be told by a succession of three or four teachers
that he must start off by being very strict. The school may not
be a 'difficult' one and yet the emphasis may be entirely on
problems of discipline and not at all on the information he
needs in order to prepare his work with the children. This kind
of induction can only serve to puzzle and confuse him. Since
staff who give such advice cannot possibly be all tough-minded
martinets we may therefore wonder why they take this particular line. It may be that any new member is seen as a potential
threat to the established group, and this kind of induction is to
make sure that he realizes that his first loyalty is to the staff
group rather than to any educational purposes he may have.
The young trained teacher, particularly, may be advised to
forget whatever idealistic nonsense he has picked up on his
education course. The model of teaching that seems to operate
here is of a conflict between teacher and child, and the new
teacher has to be shown which side to take. In our experience
in similar situations it often happens that the young teacher is
regaled with alarming accounts of rebellious classes, with
stories of teachers who have gone to the wall, and with recommendations about punitive measures which solved all problems.
The new teacher is seen as potentially the weakest part of the
solid front put up by the staff group, and it is implied that to
get the support of his colleagues he must show himself to be as
unyielding as they are, or would like to appear. He may very
well have memories from his own days at school when he took
part in playing up students or young teachers. These memories
probably contain exaggerations, but can be a source of fear,
since he may feel that his own past aggressiveness deserves
retribution. Certainly this is a feeling students often express to
us in discussion. For all of us, memories of misbehaviour in
the classroom are coloured by a kind of illicit excitement. The
idea of teaching as conflict is seductive because it appears to
resolve feelings about authority on the part of both children

and teachers. Children feel that, by their sporadic outbursts of rebelliousness, they have established their autonomy in relation to authority, while teachers, by repressing this rebelliousness, feel that they are upholding the structure of society. In neither case have the real problems of authority been faced up to realistically.

One of the criteria of a healthy group is the ability to incorporate a new member in a realistic way. It must not use him for its own irrational purposes – for example to help to fend off imaginary fears of impending chaos and destruction – but must value him for what he is. A staff group in an authoritarian school, with deep-rooted anxieties about its ability to incorporate change without dissolution, finds it very difficult to do this. It is only when the staff of the school feel secure in their relationship with authority and one another, and feel that they can afford to talk to one another freely about their educational purposes, that they can incorporate a new member constructively. Such a group will be interested to know what he brings in the way of skills ands interests, will recognize his individuality, and at the same time will acknowledge that his coming will in some degree change the way the group functions. He will not be a paragon of virtue, nor is he likely to be utterly useless. He will need help, but help can only be given where there is a habit of easy communication among the staff and where the asking for help is not seen as a sign of weakness. Isolation in the classroom is a traditional characteristic of teachers in secondary schools. It is still true in many schools that teachers rarely visit one another's classrooms to work together, and this may contribute to the difficulty they experience in general staff discussion. The staff meeting in the authoritarian school is notoriously lacking in the interchange of genuine opinion, staff are reluctant to take initiatives, and heads readily fill the silence with uninterrupted monologue. When things do go wrong in the school heads frequently deal with it unilaterally – it may be by seeing children or members of staff privately, or by calling in exercise books for a thorough scrutiny of examination and test results. Sometimes, when a young teacher's classroom is not as quiet as those in authority would like, an established member of staff may come into the room with the familiar excuse: 'I'm sorry, I didn't realize there was anyone in here.' None of these procedures is helpful, because they will all inevitably be seen by the teachers concerned as unhelpful comment on their professional capacity. When criticisms by heads and established staff are conveyed to the new teacher in these ways the whole staff group is likely to be made more rather than less anxious. This in turn will tend to decrease their capacity to communicate with one another or to be flexible enough to welcome new members. It is not surprising then that many young teachers find that their first few terms of teaching present formidable problems.

The fear of failure is a major source of anxiety to young teachers, and this failure tends to be conceived as complete and overwhelming. Yet, as every teacher knows, failure is generally specific, a matter of *part* of a lesson being unsuccessful or of a poor relationship with a *particular* class. In this sense failure is built into teaching – there is no such thing as unqualified success. Teaching is a complex activity involving relationships as well as the transmission of knowledge, and it is unlikely that a class of children ever learns the same thing at the same time or in the same way. The young teacher needs to be given help in discerning specific causes of failure or success and in generally evaluating the outcome of his work. If the kind of advice he is given on entering the school centres on keeping up the appearance of dominance over the class, he can never begin to learn what teaching really means. Success for him may become tied irrevocably to the keeping of order at whatever cost to better purposes. When we supervise teaching practice it happens not infrequently that a student tells us that a particular lesson has been an utter failure. This is generally no more realistic than the pretence that there is nothing wrong. Specific questioning about the course of the lesson and what has led up to it often helps to clarify where it has gone astray. For instance, in a lesson which has seemed chaotic, with all the class shouting out at once, there may in fact have been contributions which in less trying circumstances would have been recognized as useful leads for further work. The young teacher who hears more experienced members of staff talking realistically about the fluctuating fortunes of their lessons is in a good position to come to terms with his own occasional failures. As things are at present, it is a rare school in which the teacher who is having difficulties, of whatever kind, feels able to call in colleagues for assistance without this being seen by all concerned as evidence of failure.

It is clear from what we have said so far that we regard the proper exercise of authority in school as a highly complex matter. The climate of opinion in society at large is turning against simplistic and autocratic approaches to the transactions between the generations and many students welcome this change. Schools reflect general uncertainty about the alternatives, but they have, if they will take them, opportunities to experiment with them and to arrive at viable solutions. The young teacher enters the profession with the intention to educate rather than instruct, and to create new relationships with the children in his care. If these ideals are not to be squandered he must be helped to establish friendly relations with his classes without losing sight of the professional nature of the teacher's role. If he seeks friendship for its own sake and for his own gratification he will be unable to tolerate the inevitable rebuffs of day-to-day classroom teaching. He will tend to see them in purely personal terms and feel that he and all that he stands for has been totally rejected. These feelings are likely to deflect him from his professional purposes, and even to make it impossible for him to mobilize the teaching skills he has acquired during his training. If this process goes on unchecked he may well fall either into a self-protective appearance of indifference – 'You can't teach these children anything' – or into open hostility – 'A strong right hand is all they understand.' Only an understanding of how children, particularly the reluctant learners, see authority in its various guises and some insight into his own attitudes to authority can help the young teacher to avoid these extremes. But he cannot do it alone. The school as an institution has a part to play in the way it welcomes him into partnership with other teachers. This will only happen where the whole staff group, including the head, is engaged in continuous dialogue about the educational purposes of the school and the whole structure of authority within it.

Chapter 5
Social Class: A Clash of Values

At the heart of much of the difficulty experienced by teachers in relation to reluctant learners lie differences of social class. Most teachers, particularly graduate teachers, are middle class by origin or by attainment, while most of the children who leave school early are from working-class or lower-working-class families. As far as these admittedly crude categories go, the evidence is incontrovertible. It is curiously difficult to get students and teachers to face the implications of this fact. Some simply deny its truth, believing, hopefully, that with the spread of affluence 'we are all middle class now'. Others, less naïve, are nevertheless reluctant to engage in discussion about the matter. There is a tendency to feel that any such discussion is inevitably loaded in favour of middle-class values and involves the depreciation of every aspect of working-class life. This is not our view: what we aim at on the Hillview project is to provide students with opportunities to explore class differences, with the specific object of identifying them as possible sources of conflict. We try to increase the student's self-awareness as well as his understanding of others. The task is not made any easier by the fact that schools in outlook, and in their value systems, are essentially middle-class institutions. The school sees itself as meeting the general requirements of society, but too often these requirements become identified with what are specifically middle-class – or more properly perhaps – lower middle-class values. Membership of a social class of course does not of itself determine values and behaviour. What we are talking about are certain broad tendencies. The teacher needs to be sensitive not only to these and their effects, but also to the specific nature of individual variations.

First, we wish to consider the middle-class concern with forward planning, the tendency to renounce the present in favour of the future. There is in middle-class life an emphasis on achievement, on getting on, of being prepared to postpone immediate satisfactions in the interest of the long-term goal. Teachers, whatever their actual social origins, are for the most part people who share this outlook and have benefited from following its precepts. Their educational progress has been marked by the successful attainment of one distant and glamorous goal after another, from eleven-plus to 'O' level, to 'A' level, to graduation from college or university. The school itself is orientated in this way: success is dependent not upon immediate satisfaction but upon the ability to tolerate frustration in the interest of the future. A middle-class child, though he may not always enjoy it, is able to negotiate his way through a tedious series of exercises partly because he accepts that they will have their place in a gradually unfolding pattern of learning. He is able to see, for example, the learning of a foreign language in this way, as well as to understand that it is likely to be of value to him in his future life. His school subjects, furthermore, have meaning for him in terms of the general ambitions he and his family take for granted. Such a child may also find it reasonably easy to cooperate with the teacher and to accept the constraints of the school. In many ways the teacher will share the values of the child's parents, and so his general demeanour and expectations will be familiar to the child. For this child and his parents, conforming to middle-class patterns of behaviour is a paying proposition.

The early school-leaver is in a very different position. He will tend to be a child who looks for immediate satisfaction, unable for very long to postpone his gratification in the light of long-term aims. Moreover, his family may not understand or value the goals set by the school, and so may fail to give the support the middle-class child enjoys. When the working-class family does value education – and many do – it may not have the knowledge to give the child the specific help he needs. The school-leaver is likely to have had little share in the system of graduated rewards by which the school operates; form prizes, house points, election to responsible offices in the school. He may well be suspicious of teachers or even actively hostile to them. The young middle-class teacher may never have met children of this kind before – at best he may have come across them in the junior school before his eleven-plus success – and he may be shocked and puzzled by their apparent indifference to the values he takes for granted. Appeals to the children's self-interest, to the competitive spirit, to the obvious need to get on may all fall on deaf ears. Of course, the children's rejection of them may be due to a variety of causes, but the point here is that the teacher is often quite unaware of the part that class differences play in such conflicts of value.

Students on the Hillview project, because they were engaged in extensive and deeply felt relationships with early school-leavers, frequently experienced frustration arising from conflicts of this kind. For example, plans for activities or excursions were made, often with the collaboration of the children, but came to nothing through their inability to carry them through. It seemed for some too difficult to hold a plan in mind even from one week to the next. In these circumstances students became discouraged by the children's apparent indifference or withdrawal of interest. For example, Mr Cartwright says of his two boys:

We had arranged to meet at the bus stop at 1.30 in order to go fishing; they had been very keen and had made all the arrangements. In fact they arrived at 2 o'clock without any apology, but said that they had decided we couldn't go fishing because they hadn't got a licence. Obviously true, but also they must have known this last week when they were arranging things.

The note of irritation on Mr Cartwright's part is understandable: he may well have thought the boys' failure to plan the outing effectively a sign of fecklessness or immaturity. Yet there are so many instances among these early leavers of an inability to follow through proposals which they themselves initiate that it seems reasonable to suppose that class attitudes play some part. Most middle-class fifteen-year-old boys would have had ample opportunities for making fairly complex social arrangements, living as they do in circumstances where making plans is common and is often engaged in by the whole family together. It is difficult for students and teachers who have coped successfully with organized living to understand the genuine problems of people who tend to live from moment to moment. Our students, partly because of the relatively unstructured nature of the project, again and again came up against examples of difficulties of this kind. Mr Fry writes:

Earlier I had shown them my clarinet. Victor wouldn't have a blow but Tom risked making a fool of himself and produced some noises with great exertions, to his evident satisfaction. Victor expressed his view of the utter impossibility of his ever being able to play the clarinet. Both of them seemed to look across a great gulf at some particular accomplishment – be it playing the clarinet or going to the university – and ignore the intermediate steps which would theoretically and practically connect it with themselves. They have no will apparently to reach a distant goal – a will strong enough to carry them through the intermediate labours. . . . Tom was pleased to make some noises on the clarinet; for him that is the end of the matter; that seems to be his horizon, although to me it seems just to be the beginning.

Mr Cartwright has a sympathetic appreciation of the problem, though his own upbringing perhaps leads him to suppose that an effort of will is all that is required. The situation is more complex than that of course, yet calls upon children to exercise their willpower are not uncommon in schools. It seems not to be realized that if the goal is too distant to be meaningful appeals of this kind will certainly go unheeded. And of course those who make the appeals are then confirmed in their conviction that these children are weak of character and lacking in staying power.

One of the greatest sources of puzzlement to the students was the children's attitude to future employment. Since most of them were in their last year at school the question of the jobs they would do when they left was a frequent topic of conversation. The students are relatively ambitious people with a clear concept of the career ladder before them. They will have grown up in homes where it is taken for granted that they will eventually take up a worthwhile occupation. They themselves have no doubt been subjected to continuous questioning about what they want to be when they grow up. It is not surprising then that they ask similar questions of the children, nor that they were made uneasy by some of the answers they got. There was generally among both boys and girls an extraordinary vagueness as to their future plans, even though the school, too, clearly made efforts to get them to consider the future. The children even found ways of defending themselves against such adult pressure. As one student observed:

It seems that within the group it is important to have a job at this stage and Ken, who has not got one, said, 'I makes them up all the time.' Everyone seems to know that he is making them up – this seems to be an accepted part of the procedure.

Even when children appear to have some genuine preference for a job they were often vague about what was involved:

Doris had said she wanted to be a nanny. I asked her how and where she would train. 'I can't remember – some school or place where you become a children's nurse – I don't know where – did know but I forget.' She was not particularly worried about what she would be doing next year.

Young people's lack of precision and realism about future prospects can be a real source of anxiety for teachers. There were examples of complete fantasy, such as wanting to be a pop-singer or an air hostess, but even when the jobs mentioned were more realistic, the children had difficulties in envisaging exactly what their demands would be. In the following example this takes the form of a facile optimism:

We also talked a bit more about his future career about which he was airily confident. Of course, he would get on in the butchering trade; he would very soon get to the top. Or else he would get into the army; when he got out he could do anything he wanted. When we got to the snooker he was equally confident that he was going to win. He lost. He treated this as a minor set-back in no way corresponding to the real order of things. . . .

Many of the children were all too realistic about their prospects and sometimes surprised the students by their apparent lack of ambition. Even though they were sure that they did not wish to remain at school they had little idea of exactly what they would do. In some cases ambitions were expressed to the students at the beginning of the year, but had been abandoned without apparent cause by the end. One boy had been certain he wanted to be a butcher, but when the time came he was casually looking for some kind of employment as a mechanic. Despite the efforts of the school, many of the children finished up looking for their jobs in a most haphazard and casual way. As one of the students remarked in a tutorial discussion, 'They go round the market and woodwork places on Saturdays. They don't even look at the ads.' Having established good relations with the children, students were often distressed by the random manner in which they finally found their way into employment which might well occupy them for the rest of their working lives.

Iris has no idea what she wants to do, she will probably drift into a factory or shop and be as bored as she is at school.

This student defends herself against the pain of her realization of the futility and waste in the girl's life by an apparent acceptance of things as they are. Unfortunately this kind of defence, perhaps necessary at the time, can lead to a hardening of attitude and a denial of sensitivity. Another student, sympathetic and intelligent, came to the following dismal conclusion:

I felt no longer upset at the prospect of them working monotonous hours. I know now that the girls are quite self-sufficient. They are never worried over anything and come to think of it, that isn't a bad attitude to adopt, is it?

It is evidently a disheartening experience to be faced with this kind of apathy. It seems to deny the investment that our students, and also their teachers, have made in these children, both in terms of human relationship and in their efforts to further their educational progress. The demoralization resulting from an inability to cope with feelings of frustration may be one cause of what sometimes seems to be the abandonment of the early leavers by many schools. Too often their last year at school is merely a child-minding operation, with both teachers and pupils simply waiting for the relief of the end of the year.

A further source of concern for the students, and no doubt for many teachers too, is the kind of occupation that early school-leavers tend to take up. Many of their jobs are the kind that our society does not value highly, either because they require little skill or because they are dirty and repetitive. (As industry becomes increasingly efficient and modernized it is likely that such jobs will disappear altogether.) Although a good number of the students have limited experience of vacation work of a manual or unskilled nature, it is not usually sufficient to give real insight into the way of life that is associated with such work. Mr Upsall writes of one boy's plans:

Wally is still keen on the slaughtering business. It seems to be an actual job waiting for him. He described in some detail what he would have to do, viz. slit open cows, sheep, etc.; pull out innards; sweep up the blood and so on. When I said that I would not care to do it myself (there is an understatement tailored for the situation if you like!), he shrugged and said, 'Well, it's only a job isn't it?' and 'Someone's got to do it.'

Wally evidently relished the prospect of this job which had an element of skill and variety attached to it, but what of the monotonous dead-end jobs at an automated machine? Many of the girls from the school went to work at a cigarette factory, whatever sorts of wishful thinking they had indulged in in the early part of their leaving year. We found our students desperately searching for some compensatory virtues in the job, despite the fact that they had been very unhappy about the children's prospects at the beginning of the year. Miss Quinney said in a tutorial discussion, 'I had my doubts at first but now I think Alice will be happy there. She will have friends to talk to and besides there isn't anything else she can do.' When she said this Miss Quinney did not sound really convinced of its truth. Her words were rather the equivalent of a kind of despairing shrug of the shoulders. There is a real problem here for the sympathetic teacher: should she go on expressing doubt to these young people about the value of the work they are going to do, with the involvement in political education which this implies, or should she, as Miss Quinney does, pretend that all will be well and so effectively close the discussion? Or again, should she, as happens in some schools, ignore the whole problem as being no business of hers but the sole responsibility of the careers teacher or youth employment officer? Miss Quinney was sympathetic enough to see that the fact that some of Alice's friends were also working at the factory was of some importance to her. If the teacher is to be of any help to these young people she must have some understanding of the quality of their future working life. What might seem peripheral by-products of a middle-class career are likely to be of central importance to work in a factory: social life on the shop floor with its raillery and local mythologies, friendships and rivalries or the entertainments laid on by the management. The girl in the following tape-recording sees the provision of facilities for playing games as more important than the nature of the job:

PAULINE: Well, the youth employment officer said that there are some factories — where there are games there.

MISS CORDELL: Well, try and choose one that has. . . . Has the one that your sister works for got games?

PAULINE: I don't think so, I don't know.

MISS CORDELL: Well, I should certainly go somewhere where you can play, because when you are so good at hockey it's a pity to waste it.

PAULINE: And the youth employment officer said that if you are good at doing anything with games they might give you the day off or something like that.

The need is to help teachers to see the children's and their parents' view of work in a realistic way. It is significant that the member of staff who has the responsibility for giving information about future employment is described in most schools as the 'careers teacher'. This title already carries middle-class connotations: work is seen in terms of initial qualifications, salary scale, promotion and long-term prospects. For most early leavers the situation is very different: jobs are found casually as the need arises, often on the recommendation of parents and friends, rarely far away from home. Frequent changes of job are common; they are not necessarily evidence of fecklessness, but simply of sampling what is available. The kind of advice normally given in schools means little to these children. The students on the project remarked on the irrelevance of career pamphlets on forestry or civil engineering or nursing, all of which demanded paper qualifications certain to be out of reach for most of these children. Most of the jobs that they would do, and that their fathers were doing, had little of the self-direction that the middle-class career offers. For them a job would normally demand obedience to external pressures and proscriptions. It is not easy to see how the teacher who encourages initiative and self-direction in his pupils can honestly help them to accept the conformity that society will demand of them. (It can be argued that one of the undeclared functions of the secondary school is to ensure a ready supply of submissive and unquestioning workers – and much of what we have learned about the experience of early leavers supports the case.) However, through their close relationship with the children and through talking with them about their futures, our students began at least to have some insight into different kinds of jobs and into very different attitudes to work in general.

Just as class differences make difficulties for the teacher in matters like the planning of work in school and after, so they may cause conflict between teacher and child in matters which touch on personal interest and ways of spending leisure time. Many leisure activities seem to be chosen and approved of on class lines. In middle-class eyes tennis may be respectable while snooker is not; social life in a youth club may be all right, but meeting friends on street corners is not. It is as though teachers had selected a number of activities which they considered helpful and improving, while others are assumed to be not worthwhile. When given the opportunity by the Hillview project to choose a way of spending the afternoon with the children, our students tended initially to take them to places of cultural interest. There were visits to churches, libraries, art galleries and museums. There was a kind of missionary outlook, an attempt to interest the children in what was thought to be good for them:

Against the will of Owen we went to look at some pictures. The idea of stopping in front of a picture for several minutes was quite alien. We began at a very rapid speed, but I made him stop at some pictures and to look at them more closely. He was particularly incensed at some of the modern stuff. He could do just as well as that he said, he would not give sixpence for modern paintings.

On another occasion Miss McMullen took her charges to her flat:

Rose showed interest in my record player and asked if I had many records. When I showed her she wrinkled up her nose at the Brahms Violin Concerto. 'How can you listen to this all the time? I hates the violin.'

It was of course a proper ambition to try to introduce the children to a wider range of cultural experience. It was noticeable though, to begin with at any rate, that the assumption was that children had nothing to offer of their own. Only as the relationships developed were the students able to find some areas of interest which they could share – often essentially physical activities, swimming, ice skating and fishing. In some cases the children had more expertise in them than the students and so had the pleasure of instructing them, a pleasure it should be said that students enjoyed quite as much as the children. Some were able to share a genuine interest in pop music. On their visits to these students' flats the children were intrigued to find pop records, and were pleasantly surprised at the extent of the students' knowledge about them. Where teachers are genuinely appreciative of such a persuasive aspect of popular culture their interest can go some way towards meeting the

children on their own ground. (Where there is no such appreciation of course it would be disastrous to feign it.) There is
still a widespread dismissal of pop music by teachers on moral
and cultural grounds which are closely linked to class prejudice.
What the teacher has to do is to try to understand and accept
the importance of the role of such music in the social life of
the teenager. Unsympathetic criticism of any of their enjoyed
pursuits is very easily taken by young people as a rejection of
their whole way of life.

An unexpected obstacle to extending the children's range of
interest was their reluctance sometimes to expose themselves to
unusual pursuits for fear of failure. It seems that for some the
experience of failure in school and in other social situations
has become generalized into the expectation of lack of success
in every field. On one occasion one student and her boyfriend
had planned to take two girls ten-pin bowling for the first
time:

When it came to the girls' turn to play they blankly refused to do
so. They sat there in absolute and horrified terror. My boyfriend
thought I must have trapped them along by force to the place, but
they had been quite keen. After much fuss they played – badly at
first because self-conscious – then better later. We came out, they
were flushed with success, they had apparently enjoyed it.

Sometimes there was an additional difficulty: some of the
students must have appeared overwhelmingly competent.

Wanda said she was interested in photography the first time we
met, and was at one stage trying to get a job in a processing works,
so I expected her to show more enthusiasm towards the idea of
using the darkroom here. In practice, she became more reluctant as
time went on, and I think that reluctance was based on fear that
this would be another thing that I, with better equipment, facilities
and skill, could manage better than she.

This student shows considerable understanding here of the
discouraging effect sometimes of a too ready display of the
sorts of accomplishments that come naturally from a middle-

class upbringing. This can be a problem in the classroom too: the good teacher learns to withhold his expertise at times in order not to swamp the child's own efforts. It is all to easy to become impatient, to snatch away a book or a brush from a child who is struggling, and to demonstrate how it should be done. This is damaging enough with any child, but for the discouraged it can be disastrous. Working with such children demands considerable tact as well as knowledge and sympathy.

The intending teacher is usually someone whose leisure time has been relatively restrained and orderly, in that he has accepted the need to plan his time to meet the demands of homework or study at college or university. School and college societies have been available to him and have provided the means to direct his leisure into acceptable and constructive channels. In contrast, the early school-leaver tends to be 'unclubbable' – school societies are not for him. Even when such societies do exist the child may feel excluded by what seem to him restrictive demands in the way of performance or behaviour. Youth clubs too, with few exceptions, seem to the children to be too posh or socially demanding. Students taking part in the project were shocked to find that the children's leisure time was often spent in apparently random and sometimes destructive ways. These fifteen-year-olds commonly stood about on street corners or drifted about in groups through the shopping centre, upsetting adults and flirting with other young people. Sometimes we thought that there was an element of envy in the students' view of this, a feeling that these adolescents had more freedom and excitement than they had enjoyed themselves. But sometimes such activities were described in an unsympathetic sort of way, indicating an inability to understand what such behaviour meant in the eyes of the children. Students failed to see the connection between these forms of social behaviour and their own more formalized lives. Miss Wheeler, reporting that her girls suggested that they should visit a local dance hall, said in a disparaging tone: 'They only go there to pick up boys.' So remote were the lives of the children from her own that she was unable to connect her motives with theirs;

dancing in the Students' Union seemed to her quite a different sort of affair from a dance in the town.

Conflict is also likely to arise between the middle-class teacher and the working-class child as a consequence of their differing views about appropriate social behaviour. Propriety and good manners are an essential part of the middle-class code, and middle-class children are introduced to them at a very early age. There is no doubt that middle-class teachers find noisy and apparently unmannerly behaviour singularly distressing, whatever the circumstances. They feel called upon to correct such behaviour from motives which have strong moral overtones. The less restrained, and in some ways more direct, manners of some working-class children are often misinterpreted. For instance, a loud voice or a hearty greeting from a distance may be seen, quite wrongly, as deliberately aggressive acts directed against the teacher. Similarly, physical expressions of familiarity such as touching or pushing may not have the aggressive meaning that the more gently brought-up teacher would attribute to them. Any new situation in the school is likely to cause stress and the working-class child who has not the social acumen to help him to cope with it confidently may well resort to noisiness, laughter or other forms of 'inappropriate' behaviour. It is important for the teacher to understand the underlying cause of such behaviour, to treat its occurrence in a professional rather than a moral way, and to be wary of resorting to outraged repression.

Certainly our students were preoccupied with manners and with what seemed to them (and sometimes was!) inappropriate behaviour. Initially, the children tried to behave as they thought they ought to:

He showed tremendous courtesy and an overpowering respect for me with persistent opening of doors to let me pass. . . . I must confess I did not find this altogether displeasing, but it is an obstacle to understanding.

The student's comment showed sensitivity to the fact that good manners do not necessarily reflect warmth or consideration, that they may in fact interfere with good relations in schools. However, this 'honeymoon period' did not last long and, as the relationship between students and children developed, the students began to report more and more examples of unrestrained behaviour by the children. Although the students did not wish to be treated as though they were teachers they found it hard to tolerate some of the children's behaviour, particularly in public places:

The kids went berserk in the High Street, shouted after women, cheered a couple necking in the park and plucked flowers. 'Oh ei em terribly sorry, mey deah,' Gladys remarked when she accidentally barged into a middle-aged lady in a fur coat.

This was an extreme example of a kind of behaviour that was fairly common and that caused the students considerable embarrassment. Both students and teachers in general have behind them years of training, whether from parents or teachers, in how to behave appropriately in social situations: to sit still, to be polite to strangers, not to eat ice-cream or chips in the street and to wear the correct school uniform (one of the chief justifications of school uniforms is that it allows breaches of conduct to be readily observed!). It is not surprising that the children's uninhibited behaviour caused acute anxiety. There is a clash of values here: the early school-leavers may have learnt a code of behaviour appropriate in their home environment, but it will not necessarily coincide with the elaborate system of restraints that the middle class takes for granted. Schools are increasingly encouraged to take children out of the classroom. It is worth remembering that teachers with normal middle-class inhibitions may find these situations difficult to handle. The young teacher needs support from senior staff to help him understand the source of the children's behaviour on outings, and to cope with anxieties about his personal effectiveness.

One aspect of the restraint which middle-class people exercise is their control of physical aggression. The students on the project were quickly made aware of the amount of violence in the lives of the children. While some horseplay is permitted to students, most, by the time they have chosen their careers, have learnt to conform to non-violent standards. They are able to verbalize their aggression or postpone it until they can relieve it safely. The children were much more spontaneously aggressive, even to each other, than our students had expected. Outbursts of bad temper, and a quick resort to fighting with no regard for consequences, seemed to be commonplace behaviour in and out of the classroom. All children find it difficult to control aggressive impulses, but for many of these children such aggression among themselves was regarded as normal behaviour. Some of the girls talked to the students about the fights they had with each other. One student wrote in her journal:

Jenny has a black eye, a fight with another girl over a bag of crisps; the affair illustrates how emotional the girls are and how quickly they give way to violence.

There was among these children an extraordinary lack of shame about the open display of such emotions. There was no attempt to inhibit them in the presence of the students. On one occasion two students were returning from an outing to a chocolate factory with three boys.

It was soon clear however that Frank and Ned were allies against Jonathan. Apart from laughing at him, they started to shrow pieces of chocolate wrappers at him and, on Frank's part at least, even to spit small pieces of chocolate at his clothes. We were in the front of the van and not too well positioned to see exactly what was going on, but we clamped down when we realized. By this time Jonathan was threatening to 'lay one on the other two'.

Quarrels like this flare up easily and often seem not to give rise to rancour. This same Jonathan said to the other two soon after this incident, 'I dunno why I forgives you so often.'

On occasions students were confronted by more serious kinds of violence:

On the Sunday before, Olive was involved in a fight with another girl, the second girl had a penknife and Olive's hand was cut quite badly (she needed five stitches). This is the second serious fight she has had since I have known her.

Although few of the children were in any serious sense delinquent, a number of them were regularly involved in gang activity. Most of these gangs appear to have been rather loose associations involved in ringing doorbells, letting off bangers, and baiting park keepers and cinema ushers. A number of the boys, however, were regularly involved in gang fights, as this extract from a tape-recorded dialogue between Mr Lloyd and Arthur shows:

MR LLOYD: Well, what can you do? I have never been in a fight like this, what happens?

ARTHUR: If they gets on the floor they gets trampled on and when they gets up they just gets hit in the mouth and that.

MR LLOYD: You really hurt him?

ARTHUR: Yes, if we are only playing though, we won't hurt them. Some nights we only plays with them.

MR LLOYD: What's the difference between playing and fighting?

ARTHUR: I only comes home with one black eye!

MR LLOYD: Well, say you hit someone and they get a black eye and you are only playing, what is his reaction when you hit him?

ARTHUR: He'll probably hit us back. We don't mind it – we expects them to hit us back, then we goes on rougher.

MR LLOYD: How many people in this group you go out with?

ARTHUR: Fifteen I think – the other night we went out with fifteen. The other night we went out with nine – ten – something like that.

MR LLOYD: And you decide at school when you are going to go out at night.

ARTHUR: Yeah.

Further conversation with Arthur showed Mr Lloyd that this violent behaviour did not arise simply from unpremeditated encounters. Amongst these particular boys it was a definite part of their culture, learnt in the family and neighbourhood, which gave value and status to physical strength and the power to hold one's own in a fight.

ARTHUR: I wants a little brother so I can teach him to fight.

MR LLOYD: What sort of fighting do you teach Willie's little brother?

ARTHUR: Wrestling.

MR LLOYD: Does he ever win?

ARTHUR: No ... I lets him now and then ... so I said one day the little'un will be better than Willie.

MR LLOYD: How much difference in age is there between Willie and the little one?

ARTHUR: Five years I think ... one's six and one's eleven.

MR LLOYD: Five years and yet the younger one can beat the older one?

ARTHUR: No, he can't beat him yet, but he soon will be able to because he's got more muscles now.

MR LLOYD: And you are training the younger one.

ARTHUR: We all are round our way – the big 'uns are training the little'un because we wants him to be the hardest kid around our way.

A little later we hear Arthur being severely critical of the upbringing of one of his contemporaries:

ARTHUR: He can't fight.

MR LLOYD: So he doesn't go out?

ARTHUR: No.

MR LLOYD: Is he nice?

ARTHUR: He's all right. He's taller than I am but he ain't as strong. He was brought up wrong, his Dad wouldn't teach him how to fight.

Arthur was known as a tearaway at school and was frequently in trouble for aggressive behaviour in the classroom. Through the development of a personal relationship with the boy Mr Lloyd was able to view his behaviour with some degree of detachment. He was not frightened by or censorious of the boy's violence and so was able to allow him to talk freely about his experiences. Mr Lloyd was clearly in no sense condoning the violence, but through his questions gently trying to get the boy to consider the implications of it.

Attitudes to property and money were also the cause of misunderstanding. Completely different sets of values seemed to emerge from some of the students' comments on the spending habits of the children. One student was goggle-eyed at the amount of money one of his boys spent on fruit machines, and another commented on the generous abandon with which another boy spent the liberal supply of pocket money he carried with him. Visits to the children's homes revealed what seemed to students lavish expenditure on inessentials. In one case a large quantity of toys had been bought for a younger child in a home which was lacking some of the basic necessities. Several of the families bought gadgets which were never put into anything like full use; for example, a tape-recorder played with at the Christmas party but tucked away for the rest of the year. Students brought up with middle- or lower-middle-class views on saving, on value for money, and with a generally prudent attitude to property and money find it difficult simply to accept differences. Too often they, in common with many older teachers, slip into moralistic judgements where these are quite inappropriate. The danger of a moralistic outlook is that it may distort the middle-class adult's perception of the behaviour of the children. One student describes some of the boys as mercenary because of their speculations about the value of the objects they came across in their outings: 'The lead in the Roman baths, coins, the ornaments in the abbey were all seen as objects of cash value and assessed.' When the same student visited a packing-plant with the boys, he described one of them as 'mercenary' because he asked about wages and hours. Really this was a sensible and practical inquiry.

Stealing is common among adolescents of all social classes. Although the activity is identical, middle-class and working-class children have different feelings about it. It is dangerous to generalize about such a private activity, but our impression is that for most middle-class children stealing is only an occasional event, accompanied by strong feelings of guilt. The experience is often 'forgotten' and seems not to come readily to mind when the problem of children's stealing is discussed. For working-class children, especially for boys, stealing or 'knock-

ing off' is a seemingly casual affair, and provided that the stealing is not done from friends is socially tolerated or even
encouraged. The only time shame is experienced is when a
theft is discovered and brought to public notice. The Hillview
project brought students face-to-face with the realization that
many of the children they were becoming fond of were given
to petty thievery – and in some cases more serious offences
than that. They found it difficult to know how to deal with this
knowledge, particularly as in the following incident, when it
appeared to happen in their very presence. Miss Knight writes
in her journal:

Anyway we went to the boutique and I kept a careful eye on them
while they tried on jewellery. We had already been warned by the
class teacher that shoplifting might occur, but I did not think that
either of them would take anything. The boutique must be a shop-
lifter's paradise – everything lying about and hardly an assistant in
sight. We had spent an hour almost wandering through every
department. Doreen had admired some soft toys and I had offered
to help them make some if they wanted to. Then Doreen saw some
very tiny hedgehogs made from wood and fur at the ridiculously
high price of 6s. 11d. She said she wanted one for her mother, but
thought that the price was far too high and could not afford it. Vera
had started to dismantle one of those sets of Russian dolls made up
from one doll placed inside another – she was getting in a muddle
trying to put them back so, leaving Doreen playing with the hedgehogs, I turned around to help Vera. A sudden movement from
Doreen caught my eye; she was standing with her back to me looking towards the assistant who was busy at the end of the shop. Her
hand was quickly thrust into her blazer pocket. A feeling of panic
came over me – I could not be sure whether she had taken anything,
her actions were certainly suspicious. Vera appeared not to have
noticed anything and Doreen certainly had not seen me looking.
Should I have said anything to her? It was the element of doubt
which held me back. I did not want to wrongly accuse her of taking
anything, thus probably ruining our relationship at this early stage.
Girls at this age can be so sensitive to criticism. From that moment
it seemed as though a black cloud had descended over the afternoon.
I don't know if they had noticed any change in my behaviour, but I
was almost frantic with worrying whether I should have said any-

thing to her. We had already been warned that this might happen. You think of all the things you can do or say if and when such an incident happens but when it does you are taken so unawares that it becomes a different matter.

We came out of the shop almost immediately. It was I who felt guilty, expecting to be grabbed by an assistant as I was going through the door.

If she did take a hedgehog why did she do it? As she already said, because she wanted one and they were too expensive for her? I'll probably never know. I am now wondering whether I should forget the matter or mention something about shoplifting in the near future. It would have been a different matter if I had actually caught her with the hedgehog in her hand. Though I cannot honestly say what I would do in such a situation.

Doreen was in a very great hurry to go home as soon as we had left the shop. I could not help wondering if she had not after all seen me looking at her! I wonder if she will turn up next week.

Several things emerge from this complex situation. First, as with many of the students, Miss Knight does not want to spoil her relationship with Doreen. Second, this is a public place and any confrontation on the spot would have caused her great embarrassment. But thirdly, and most relevantly here, what to the child may be a fairly routine event is a source of considerable unease and confusion to Miss Knight. Her own upbringing will hardly have prepared her to understand so casual an attitude to 'public property'.

Unacknowledged feelings about class play a larger part in the relationship between teacher and child than is generally recognized. Attitudes towards manners, towards the expression of feeling, towards aggressiveness and property tend to be learnt in the family and are peculiarly deep-rooted. Normally these feelings are unexamined, but in any professional setting, where contact between different social classes is inevitable, it is essential that they should not remain so. The young teacher needs to explore his own attitudes and their origin, and to train himself to examine his reaction to other social classes so that he may be better able to be objective about the behaviour of children who might otherwise remain disturbingly incomprehensible. He must learn to discriminate between behaviour that is socially divisive or personally destructive and behaviour that is just different. Violence and the inability to plan, for example, are aspects of behaviour which can hardly be tolerated in a school community, while different standards of tidiness and manners can perfectly well coexist. Working-class qualities such as a more open expression of feelings could even make a positive contribution to the way our schools are run. Teachers are necessarily involved in bringing about changes in behaviour. In our society some of the values of the middle class have a general validity and it is the teacher's business to transmit them. This may be done brutally and with the heavy hand of thoughtless authority. But it can be done sensitively and with a considerate and professional concern for the child's own culture. If teachers are to teach the less able working-class child happily and effectively, and if the children are to benefit from their education, this is the way it must be done.

Chapter 6
Language: Talking Together

The establishment of a relationship between teacher and child, the way the authority of the teacher is exercised, the way members of different social classes represent the world to themselves: in all of these issues the importance of language is evident, and it is on language that we propose to focus attention in this chapter.

The setting up of an effective working dialogue between teacher and child demands some understanding by the teacher of the role of language in all development. It is not simply a matter of being familiar with regional or class differences at the level of dialect or accent, though these are not unimportant. It is rather an acceptance of the fact that the language we learn to speak in effect shapes our experience. Through the terms that it makes available to us we learn to see the world and to think about it. Talking with others is not only a means of conveying information or of simple sociability, it is one of the ways in which we structure reality and learn to find our place in the world. Through informal conversation we are enabled to articulate feeling and opinion, testing our own perceptions against those of others. We progress through talk by successive reformulations of past experience in the light of the new. In all that we say we present something of ourselves, expressing a unique view of the world. In more formal kinds of discussion, too, 'communication' is only one of the functions of the language used. It is not simply that each participant contributes information or opinion, but that as the result of hearing the contribution of others each has to restructure in some measure his own. Talk may, for example, stimulate him to shape into words personal experience which until that moment has lain dormant. As each contribution is considered, questioned or modified the participants in the discussion may arrive at some consensus about the matter in hand. While all this is happening one or more of the speakers may well make contributions which are really concerned with matters outside the apparent frame of reference: in establishing themselves as competent members of a new group for instance, or with re-establishing old ties. In much of the discussion in school the teacher will be concerned not only to encourage children to exchange personal experiences and opinions but, starting from there, to help them to arrive at valid generalization. This after all is a part of secondary education. Anything which interferes with children and teachers together engaging in meaningful talk will seriously undermine the educational intentions of the school.

From the written comments of some of the children involved in the Hillview project it is evident that they valued very highly the opportunity to talk informally with the students. They were invited by their class teacher to write about the chief differences between students and teachers as they saw them:

GIRL: With the students you feel you can talk more freely with them, and also because they treat us as friends and talk to us like friends. We also treat them like friends and we get on all right. They treat us like adults instead of how the teachers treat us. With the students they seem to trust us whereas the teachers don't.

BOY: They do not threaten you with the cane and they will treat you normally.

GIRL: They treat us more grown up than the teachers do. Also speak more nicer to us.

All these comments show how important to the children is the sense of being appreciated as persons in their own right. There is an emphasis on being treated as 'grown up', as 'adult' and as being spoken to 'normally'. For these early leavers the expressive and personal features of talk were especially significant. They particularly valued the opportunity their students gave them to affirm, through talk, their own individuality. The circumstances in which they met the students, informally and usually in small groups, encouraged such an affirmation. The teacher in the classroom, faced with large numbers and the demands of a structured curriculum, has a much more difficult task.

Not that informal talk came easily, even in the more favourable circumstances provided by the Hillview project. Many of the students, engaged as they were in the process of learning the roles of the teacher, found it difficult to avoid the didactic mode, however inappropriate it was. Mr Gillow in the following extract from his journal shows that he encountered this difficulty:

Keith and I visited the castle in pursuance of his interest in history. On reaching the museum there he told me he had already been some time ago, but was quite willing to cooperate with my wish to make the visit. We wandered from room to room, Keith showing particular interest in agricultural implements. He has an uncle with a farm in Herts which he has visited. We discussed the great advances in technological spheres over the last hundred years in comparison with previous historical methods of farming which had remained virtually similar for centuries. Keith was also interested in the old methods of torture and poacher-catching devices, etc.; he was able to recall some of the exhibits from his previous visit and to say a little about them. We then visited the keep, which Keith knew. He was able to show me the way up to it and to demonstrate the impressive view from the top. During the afternoon we discussed a wide variety of topics, such as ancient history, education, his science lessons, parents and space travel, world poverty and politics. Most of these discussions consisted of me giving my opinions and Keith either agreeing or disagreeing, together with a short comment from him. He appeared to be interested in all this and seems to have a wide range of sympathies, but is constantly held back by his chronic inability to form articulate sentences or a succession of remarks.

We get a clear picture here of a teacher who is trying seriously, even desperately, to involve the boy in an educative dialogue. His very anxiety leads him, according to his own account, to flood the boy with a wide range of topics and information at too abstract a level. The boys' interests are in the concrete and immediate: the farming tools, instruments of torture and the view from the keep. Mr Gillow does not seem able to share Keith's enthusiasm at the boy's own level, nor can he allow himself simply to enjoy Keith's individuality. It is as though, in his role of teacher, he regards ordinary conversation as trivial and of no consequence, yet is in only through the exchange of immediate and personal expressions of feeling and opinion that the ground for discussion can be laid. Keith needs to feel that Mr Gillow appreciates what he says for the light it throws on who he is. Only then can he be expected to commit himself to the kind of extended comment that the student expects of him. Since the boy's level of operation is by-passed Mr Gillow can only move swiftly from one 'topic' to another. He realizes that there is something wrong, that the dialogue never really gets off the ground, but he is unable to diagnose the cause of the problem. He suggests that it is Keith's 'chronic inability to form articulate sentences' which is the root of the difficulty. The fact is that the kind of informal talk that is appropriate to this sort of situation is rarely carried on in fully formed sentences, even by well-educated adults. The tape-recorder has shown us how far from the ordered sequences of the written language talk really is. Where both parties to a dialogue share the same experience there is much that need not be made explicit. What to an observer may seem fragmentary and incoherent may to the participants be sufficient to sustain both the relationship and the dialogue. In the early stages of any relationship, particularly, one expects to find an emphasis upon talk whose primary function is to enable each party to affirm his own individuality and to become aware of the other's. Of course it is right in schools that teachers concern themselves with helping children to move through talk to some more objective view of experience, but this concern cannot be carried through when the initial starting-points which children offer are not valued or developed.

On the Hillview project we encourage students to use tape-recorders as a way of helping them to become more aware of the nature of talk and more critical of their own ability to engage in it fruitfully. Two weeks after the excursion to the castle Mr Gillow and Keith visited a church and recorded what they said as they went along. Mr Gillow writes:

Keith carried the instrument and operated it himself throughout the visit, playing the part of the recorder to my 'roving report' with evident glee, occasionally interjecting comments of his own, but more usually only responding when direct questions were asked. He did not like the 'playback', being very conscious of his own voice and vocabulary deficiency as compared with me. I do not consider it advisable, as sometimes suggested, to talk down to him or to deliberately talk his language – this, unless I was a supremely accomplished actor, would immediately create a feeling of insecurity in him, resulting from an awareness of my policies. Better to be ourselves and attempt to find common ground in mutual interests.

The last sentence here suggests that Mr Gillow has some sensitivity to what is needed. He is anxious not to present himself as other than he is. He seems, however, to see any attempt to discover what Keith is really interested in or to pick up cues from what he says as 'talking down' and necessarily insincere. Yet an adult can only get alongside any child by at least temporarily putting aside his own demanding standards and entering imaginatively into the child's experience. It is not a question of talking the child's language in the sense of imitating his accent or vocabulary, but of picking up and developing the ways of thinking and feeling that his words reveal. The teacher cannot afford to take the passive role in this transaction; it is part of his professionalism to take the initiative in establishing the contact.

Mr Gillow's over-concern with the external aspects of speech – 'voice and vocabulary' – is shared by many, both parents and teachers; and sometimes by the children themselves. For instance, some of the children expressed the fear that they did not know how to speak properly. Such self-doubts about not having the right accent, an attitude learnt perhaps from parents, certainly from some teachers, can be crippling in their effects. There is still some prejudice about accent and 'correct grammar', but the fear of opening one's mouth and revealing social inferiority can do nothing but make matters worse. The only way anyone learns to communicate more widely and in more complex ways is by doing so. Anything which inhibits this is harmful. As we have already suggested, prejudices about the externals of speech are sometimes learnt by the children themselves. Miss Upton on the following tape-recording has just learnt that Hugh's step-sister is at university while he, of course, plans to leave school as soon as he can:

MISS UPTON: You didn't tell me that before.

HUGH: Well, no need to.

MISS UPTON: Oh, interesting though.

HUGH: She was headgirl of the Vale School.

MISS UPTON: Was she?

HUGH: Yeah.

LAURIE: Headgirl!?

MISS UPTON: Where's the Vale?

LAURIE: It's the highest school in the city for girls. You know, poncy school isn't it? Only your sister wasn't poncy.

HUGH: She is.

MISS UPTON: Oh, she is is she?

HUGH: Yeah ... she speaks all wrong.

MISS UPTON: How does she speak then?

HUGH: All poncy!

MISS UPTON: How does someone speak poncy? Do I speak poncy?

HUGH: No (laughter).

MISS UPTON: Oh, saved from that then! Give me an imitation of somebody speaking poncy.

LAURIE: Oh ... (laughter) ... he don't know hisself.

HUGH (exaggeratedly): 'Oh dash it old boy' and all that.

MISS UPTON: Have you ever heard anyone speak like that?

HUGH: No.

MISS UPTON: I don't know, some people speak like that naturally because that's the way their families always spoke.

HUGH: Yeah and all those lords and all that.

MISS UPTON: Well, I don't know about them. There are people I know who speak like that at university and it's quite natural to them, you don't mind it, it doesn't grate on your nerves.

Quite apart from self-doubts engendered by social prejudice, some of the Hillview children found any kind of extended talk difficult, even with a friendly adult. Many of the students have commented on this in their journals. Subsequently developments have shown that this inarticulacy is to some extent a function of the relationship: as mutual confidence increases talk develops. However, some children said very little during the whole year and there are many examples of the difficulty others found in satisfactorily completing any extended utterance no matter how much they tried. In the following conversation Mr Jeffreys and Ted are planning what they should do next; Ted is keen to discuss the possibility of making a film, and recalls a recent experience that he thinks is relevant:

MR JEFFREYS: How can you do that? Do you know?

TED: No I don't ... um ... like make a cartoon, have you thought about that?

MR JEFFREYS: How could we do that?

TED: Oh, just make it out of cardboard. That's what ... um ... like when I was in the scouts, these two ... er ... two ... er ... scoutmasters took me home and they had, oh, like a room, you know ... er ... like this, this size, like going up into the attic, like ... um .. reels and reels of, you know, film, going all round the room, like pictures like they'd taken, pictures of the ... (*breaks down*). Then ... er ... one of the cartoons I've seen ... it wasn't a very long one, he was walking along the beach ... then he walked along a bit further ... and there's ... er ... a lady riding along on a donkey ... he stops ... faints ... starts walking along on his hands ... and following the woman ... well, I suppose that's all right ... about ... do you reckon those ... er ... those fifty new pence are any good?

There are features in this extract which are common to most relaxed talk. Hesitations marked here by 'um', 'er', or an ellipsis are not in themselves indicative of linguistic inadequacy. But there are some features which perhaps reveal an inability to sustain an account of a personal experience which has excited him. He is motivated by the student's interest to venture on this, but finds himself unable to give any coherent description of the layout of the scoutmasters' room, and breaks down when he tries to be more specific about the films they had made. He shifts then to telling the story of a cartoon film without making clear its connection with what has gone before, and again abruptly breaks off to introduce the quite new topic of decimal coinage. Boys like Ted, who find difficulty in keeping going in relatively informal circumstances, may well be reluctant even to embark on any more demanding situations involving talk.

The students on the Hillview project were encouraged from the beginning to regard talk between them and the children as of basic importance. Frequent opportunity to talk with adults was the most obvious value of the scheme for these young school-leavers – their teachers readily agreed that this was so. Yet, as we have already suggested, there were difficulties. There were occasions, for instance, when students became conscious of using words and expressions in their conversation which were unlikely to be understood. One wrote wrily:

Whilst Dick was telling me about his girlfriend (who is in the pantomime) I asked if she was 'of long standing' – which dumbfounded him! – not unnaturally.

More seriously, the strain on students when their children did not respond at all can be imagined. Through being asked to write their reflections on the weekly meetings, and through the weekly tutorial discussions, the students were helped to consider the reasons for the children's reluctance and to discover what they could about the conditions when talk could take place. Miss Hillier wrote in her journal on the occasion of her fourth meeting with Ann and Norma:

Ann and Norma wanted to go for a walk into the country. We talked a lot more than before. I feel we are getting to know each other more with each week, but it is difficult for them to relax and talk about *themselves*. I think that neither is used to giving freely direct information about themselves – probably because they have never been asked. They seem strangely without any background of experience – I have mentioned before how school and home seem just to 'happen' without their being a part of it. I still do not really feel that I have yet discovered what would bring them out to talk more freely.

Not unexpectedly, students generally found, in the early stages of their relationship at any rate, that talk did not come easily in the ordinary face-to-face setting. It was more likely to happen when they and the children were engaged in some joint activity. Miss Hillier in the above extract has at least broken down some of the barriers and the girls talked more freely as they all walked along side by side. The girls are still comparatively reticent about themselves and their own experience, partly, it seems to her, because they have no reason to believe that what they do or feel is of any consequence. Such an interpretation seems very probable when one considers how children like these tend to be undervalued, albeit unintentionally, because of differences which have put them outside the purposes of the school. Again and again we have found that when students were able genuinely to value the children, their experience and their accomplishments, talk became easier and more meaningful. For example, this is Miss Oxley's comment on the occasion when she went swimming with her two girls in the school's pool:

A remarkable thing happened! Fiona, who had hardly spoken at our previous meeting and who seemed uninterested in my suggestions – including swimming – she even told me that she couldn't swim – changed considerably. She became quite talkative, although not to the extent of Teresa, and she seemed to enjoy herself in the water. Not only that, I discovered that she could swim a breadth of the pool. When she thought no one was looking she would practise swimming, and when I lost the rubber band off my hair I turned round to see her holding her nose trying to look under water for the rubber band. I was delighted that she would talk to me. We threw a ball to each other for a couple of minutes and this I think pleased her because she had my attention to herself all this time.

Fiona is pleased that she can demonstrate an accomplishment and that she can capture the appreciative interest of Miss

Oxley, who in turn is delighted that this very reticent child begins to talk. A relationship based on mutual enjoyment rather than upon the formal operation of adult–child roles is the best ground for the establishment of a genuine dialogue. From such a beginning where the child can affirm her individuality there is hope for further development. The possibility of using talk to develop the relationship, to plan future action, to reflect upon mutual experience, has been established. It is not that from such a beginning progress will follow automatically. There will be fluctuations in the flow of talk between teacher and child, and each will discover obstacles in the other related to personality and experience and to the nature of the task in hand. Yet, once begun, the dialogue can be fostered and made to contribute to more complex understandings.

In the following, more extended, situation Mr Tunney and his three charges have to talk together to get themselves out of difficulty. The effort involved seems to lead to a real breakthrough in terms of good communication:

At the foot of the cliff Steve pointed to a spot where he claimed it would be best to climb. 'Christ, we'll never get up there!' I thought. It looked easier on the upstream side of the bridge, and crashing through some bushes we began the ascent, in almost undignified haste. I began to get worried. My shoes were slipping on the smooth rock, and the three lads were forging ahead, each in a different direction. But they were showing great enthusiasm to get on with the climb, and I didn't want to dampen this any more than I had to. Halfway up we all came together and agreed that the climb was going to be more difficult than we had imagined at first. What to do? None of them wanted to admit failure and return to the road, and besides this might have been more dangerous than to continue on up. We sat and discussed the best route to the top; which gully in the rock would be our best bet? A zigzag course looked the most hopeful, and Jake shot off along it, only to find that it had led to a sheer face with no foot or hand holds. Everybody down again, and a further discussion of our next step. All the time the suggestions were coming from them, and eventually we found a circuitous route which brought us to our objective. The whole exercise had been an object lesson in group work. Together we had discussed the problem, thought it out and carried it through to a conclusion, each individual and the group as a whole gaining in confidence all the time. Gradually the barriers between us had broken down and we were able to work together as a group. Now we were able to talk together much more freely. They started to talk about their families – Martin comes from a family of eleven, all under eighteen, Steve from a family of nine, of which, I believe, he is the eldest. Jake's family numbers five. I found out that all intended to leave at fifteen, which in Jake's case will be next Easter. Altogether a very useful afternoon. They seem to accept me more now as a friend rather than as a teacher.

While there is no doubt about the reality of this success, it is perhaps worth recording that four weeks later Mr Tunney was in a state of despondency about the relationship between him and the boys. Progress with the children on the Hillview project was rarely without setbacks.

It is not easy deliberately to engineer such real-life situations as Mr Tunney's escapade on the cliff-face, and in the context of school there will be few situations requiring so urgent a practical solution. However, on many occasions students engaged the children in conversation while sitting round at home or playing with a tape-recorder. As might be expected, talk tended then to take the form of a question-and-answer kind of dialogue. The adult in such a position, anxious to hear what the child has to say, takes the initiative and naturally asks questions. This approach is much more complex than one might at first suppose, for what is intended to be dialogue may easily become a rather unproductive sort of interrogation, as in this tape-recorded extract:

MR IBBOTSON (*of a travel book he is holding*): It actually tells you where the names of places are. All the pictures towards the front – you see, that's the end of the pictures – all the pictures towards the front . . .

CHRISTOPHER: Been there!

MR IBBOTSON: Been there? Where's that?

CHRISTOPHER: Pembrokeshire.

MR IBBOTSON: Pembrokeshire? When was that?

CHRISTOPHER: When we went with the school.

MR IBBOTSON: Oh, when – you've told me about that, haven't you? You've told me about that, haven't you?

CHRISTOPHER: er...

MR IBBOTSON: When, yes...

CHRISTOPHER: Yeah ... er ... we went for a week, er, down Wales.

MR IBBOTSON: Yes.

[later]

MR IBBOTSON: Harlech's down here, near this bit of Wales.

CHRISTOPHER: Yes.

MR IBBOTSON: That's where all the mountains, Snowdon and so on ...

CHRISTOPHER: Yeah, yeah, we climbed Snowdon.

MR IBBOTSON: You climbed up Snowdon?

CHRISTOPHER: And Tryffyn.

MR IBBOTSON: Did you now? How long did it take you to climb up Snowdon?

CHRISTOPHER: Oh, quite a long time.

MR IBBOTSON: A whole day more or less?

CHRISTOPHER: Yeah, then we went to ... er ... went round town and that, after we went to the castle.

MR IBBOTSON: Yes, yes. Did you meet anyone speaking Welsh?

Mr Ibbotson bombards Christopher with questions, never allowing or helping him to develop his answer, sometimes even managing to convey incredulity that he had achieved anything. Mr Ibbotson, as may be imagined, found it a painful experience to listen to the tape-recording with his tutor. He realized, perhaps for the first time, that some of the responsibility for difficulty in communication between himself and Christopher was his. Yet at the same time he was able to examine and to discuss the way the dialogue went, and to acquire some understanding of the skills he would need to develop talk in a constructive way. We have found that asking the students to transcribe some of their conversations with children and then to discuss them with a tutor has sometimes helped them in this way.

Much of the communication between teacher and child in

the school context will develop from questioning by the teacher. His adult role vis-à-vis the child seems to demand that he should initiate conversation, and the question form comes most easily. The questions asked can be of many kinds – it is certainly possible to ask questions which are genuinely open, enabling the child to develop his own line of thought, to present himself as he really is. When, though, this does not happen the dialogue can quickly become as stultifying as the example we have given, with the consequence that the teacher may be tempted to shift into monologue, abandoning any possibility of two-way communication. In the end, the failure to achieve any genuine dialogue will lead to stalemate or open conflict: the children will become dumb, the teacher reduced to shouting. The teacher, particularly of less able children, needs as part of his professional expertise to become skilled in the strategies of conversation and to realize that notions of 'precision', 'articulacy', 'fluency' or 'social ease' represent a much simplified view of the matter. A better knowledge of the nature and function of language will help him to realize how important it is to listen and to recognize the intention to communicate in the child's halting, partial utterance. He will have to tolerate silences which may indicate slower modes of thinking rather than a reluctance to engage. Such skills are not easily learnt, and certainly their exercise in the classroom with large groups of thirty or more represents a formidable undertaking. The Hillview project provided a setting where student teachers could at least begin to practise some of their skills and, after reflection and discussion perhaps, to improve their techniques.

Alan was a quiet boy, who tended to be overshadowed by his friend Trevor. He generally had little to say to Mr Hewitt except when he could get him to himself. On this occasion Mr Hewitt began by showing Alan a book about North America with pictures of the prairies, of combine harvesters and other machinery.

MR HEWITT: Now that's the sort of farm machinery that you would have. Those are big – um – they're called combines – um – which do all the – they cut the – er – wheat, and they – put it into bags ... (*waits for thirteen seconds for a response.*) You're sorry you're not leaving school at – um – at Christmas?

ALAN: No I can't.

MR HEWITT: No, but you're sorry you're not ...

ALAN: Um ...

MR HEWITT: Would you like to?

ALAN: It's all right at school sometimes, but I'd rather go to work, I think.

MR HEWITT: Why is that?

ALAN: I don't know – I just – I don't think I like school.

MR HEWITT: Is there anything particularly you don't like about it?

ALAN: Some of the teachers ...

MR HEWITT: Mm ... (*Four seconds wait.*) They make life difficult?

ALAN: Mm ... Especially Mr West. I don't have he no more.

MR HEWITT: Why is that?

ALAN: Well he was all right at times – whenever he was in a good mood. But when he was in bad mood he was terrible.

MR HEWITT: Mm. (*Three seconds wait.*) What does he teach?

ALAN: Geography.

MR HEWITT: You still do geography?

ALAN: Not now – I had three years of that.

MR HEWITT: Mm ... mm. (*One second wait.*) What about the others? Are they not – are there not some – Mr Moody, for example ...

(*Mr Hewitt had met Mr Moody.*)

ALAN: He's all right ...

MR HEWITT: Yeap ... nice man ...

ALAN: Mm.

MR HEWITT (*three seconds wait*): If you had teachers like Mr Moody would you – would you want to stay on?

ALAN: No, I'd rather go to work.

MR HEWITT: Mm. (*Three seconds wait.*)

ALAN: See this year is sort of different to the other ones. We've been doing lessons last year but we weren't never using them ...

MR HEWITT: Yeah.

ALAN: ... like –

MR HEWITT: And now you're doing things which are useful?

ALAN: Yep – like we're going places and – an – doing things like art and metal work, you know, what will help you when you leave school like.

MR HEWITT: Yep.

ALAN: Last year I think we had three periods of art in – um – two weeks.

MR HEWITT: Mm.

ALAN: No, three periods of metal work in two weeks.

MR HEWITT: Yep. What's the difference between art and metal work?

ALAN: Art, in one part of it you have paintings, like drawings and in – um – the other part you make – um – a pot of clay.

MR HEWITT: Do you enjoy both of these things?

ALAN: No, I like pot – um – metal work, that's not too bad.

MR HEWITT: Yeah . . . well, if this year is a better year, you know, if you're doing things that you like doing – um – would you stay on? Say last year was like this year, do you think you would stay on?

ALAN: No, well, if I weren't in this class now – say I was in one up – but they wanted me – because – um – for leavers – they'd be doing more work like French or things like that for GCEs and O-levels.

MR HEWITT: Uh um – and did you not want to do this or –

ALAN: No.

Perhaps the most noteworthy feature of this dialogue is Mr Hewitt's capacity to listen and to wait for Alan's responses. He is able to tolerate silence, by no means an easy thing to do. Silences and an apparent reluctance to join in the conversation can seem threatening, but Mr Hewitt is relaxed enough to interpret them effectively. The dialogue opens with a comment by Mr Hewitt on some pictures of farm machinery. He pauses to allow Alan to contribute if he can – the pause lasts a full thirteen seconds before he decides that this topic is not meaningful, and so shifts to one nearer the boy's immediate concerns. The next pause comes when Alan is attempting to be more specific about his dislike of school. He begins with the words 'some of the teachers . . .', but finds it difficult to formulate the generalization, and after waiting for four seconds Mr Hewitt sympathetically tries to help him with the suggestion 'they make life difficult?' He seems correctly to have interpreted Alan's hesitation, for, though he cannot continue the generalization, he does recall a specific relevant case and volunteers some further information. ('Especially Mr West. I don't have he no more.') In the ensuing exchanges Mr Hewitt several times refrains from leaping in to fill any pauses, and is finally rewarded when, for the first time in the dialogue, Alan initiates an utterance for himself. It comes when he replies, to a question from Mr Hewitt about whether he wants to stay on at school, 'No, I'd rather go to work.' Mr Hewitt seems to feel that Alan has more to say and waits patiently. Alan then speaks again and introduces a quite new aspect of the topic in his longest utterance up to that point, beginning with the words 'See this year is sort of different . . .' From that point onwards the dialogue appears to flow more easily, though Alan still needs sympathetic support to sustain his train of thought. Mr Hewitt recognizes the appeal in Alan's use of the word 'like' and is sufficiently sensitive to his intentions to help him without being too directive. Sometimes all that is needed is a 'yep' or an 'mm', supporting noises which express interest but do not divert the speaker with new information or opinions. (This is an interview technique common to therapeutic work, and one which is likely to be of value to teachers, particularly of less articulate children.)

Mr Hewitt does on occasions ask directive questions intended for the most part to encourage Alan to be more specific about events or feelings. One of the chief characteristics of the language of less able children is that they tend to make relatively undifferentiated statements about experience. The resources of language to specify and categorize the different aspects of reality are under-used and experience itself remains confused and unrelated. Mr Hewitt rightly sees it as one of his tasks to help Alan to use words to sort out this confusion. He attempts it at the very beginning of the extract when he tries to get Alan to articulate his feelings about having to stay on at school until Easter. From previous conversations he knows that the boy is anxious to leave, but now he finds he is reluctant to commit himself to a definite expression of feeling. 'You're sorry you're not leaving school' Mr Hewitt says, but Alan refuses to admit it and shifts his ground with the remark 'I can't.' Mr Hewitt repeats the point – '. . . but you're sorry you're not' – and again Alan refuses to be drawn and Mr Hewitt has to rephrase the question quite differently. Later in the extract he asks another perhaps rather more schoolmasterly question in an attempt to get Alan to differentiate between the experiences offered in some of his schoolwork. 'What's the difference between art and metal work?' Alan tries but is quite unable to use words to hold apart in his mind the two activities and to compare their characteristics. He begins with the word 'Art' which helps him to define one part of the experience he is considering; he then distinguishes the two sorts of activity it contains, painting and drawing and making 'a pot of clay'. He seems to feel that he has completed what he has set out to do, but in fact does not specify at all the nature of metal work.

Despite Alan's inability to structure his experience of school through the leads that Mr Hewitt provides, he does eventually achieve some sort of conclusion. Mr Hewitt's concern throughout has been to try to help the boy to particularize those aspects of his experience of school life which give him satisfaction, as a means of getting him to consider staying on at school for another year. He picks up Alan's remark that this year is different from the others in that it contains more practical activities, and invites him to imagine a further year of the same kind: 'Say last year was like this year, do you think you would stay on?' Alan is unable to conceive of this hypothesis, but proposes another of his own which is more concrete and narrower in its scope. He begins with the conditional clause 'if I weren't in this class now', breaks down, starts again and, with a parenthesis on the way, concludes with a statement of the school work he would have to do if he were to stay on – 'they'd be doing more work like French or things like that for GCEs and O-levels.' This is very specific and clearly implies a definite point of view, though even now Mr Hewitt has to encourage him to be explicit about his attitude.

On another occasion Mr Hewitt was talking with Alan's

friend Trevor about a boy who was in trouble with the school for not having his hair cut. In this extract Mr Hewitt moves from simple questioning to establishing a genuine dialogue, and by his patience and persistence helps the boy to arrive at an insightful generalization:

MR HEWITT: Was he asked to stay away from school?

TREVOR: No, no.

MR HEWITT: Why do you think you were asked to stay away from school?

TREVOR: I ain't been asked, not yet.

MR HEWITT: Oh, you're expecting this?

TREVOR: Yeah – soon!

MR HEWITT: Well what will happen – what will you expect to happen?

TREVOR: Um ... he'll tell me I have to have it cut and I won't have it cut. He'll say – you know – 'You won't be able to come to school unless you get it cut.' Then I'll tuck it all in me coat, underneath me collar, so it looks like it's only growing on me collar.

MR HEWITT: You can do that all right.

TREVOR: Yeah.

MR HEWITT: Say he says 'Take off your coat!'

TREVOR (*laughs*): It will be too bad then won't it. (*Laughs.*)

MR HEWITT (*laughs*): So you just get – do you get the cane for that?

TREVOR: Yeah, I don't think that's right though – I don't think it's right.

MR HEWITT: Well, this is the problem isn't it? Um – *he* thinks it's right.

TREVOR: Yeah but – er ...

MR HEWITT: Maybe the same thing – if you're – if you're working and your boss says, um, 'Take that load of stuff and put it in the lorry', and you don't think it's right, Trev – what happens?

TREVOR: You get the sack ...

MR HEWITT: Yeah? ...

TREVOR: Yeah. But you know you're expected to do that because that ain't a part of you, is it, and your hair *is* a part of you.

MR HEWITT: Oh, I see. Yes this is true – it is.

The tone of the whole dialogue is both relaxed and purposeful. The student begins with questions to establish exactly what has happened, and then invites Trevor to think about the future – 'what will you expect to happen?' Trevor first considers the question seriously and foresees quite realistically the probable series of events. He represents the headmaster's words dramatically, but at the point when he realizes the likelihood of a direct confrontation between the head and himself he slips into a fantasy solution: 'Then I'll tuck it all in me coat, underneath me collar, so it looks like it's only growing on me collar.' Mr Hewitt accepts the humour of this, enjoying with Trevor its elaboration, but at the same time uses it to impel him to consider the situation more deeply. Trevor accepts the challenge and forcibly expresses his view of the morality of the imagined beating: 'I don't think that's right though – I don't think it's right.' Mr Hewitt then faces him with the dilemma of anyone in the position of having to accept legitimate authority. He presents Trevor with an analogy drawn from a work situation he is likely to be familiar with and again asks him to consider what would be likely to happen. Trevor sees very clearly what would happen, then seems as though he might be about to make a further point. Encouraged by Mr Hewitt, he goes on to reject the validity of the analogy and makes a clear statement about where for him the proper exercise of authority ends: 'But you know you're expected to do that, because that ain't a part of you, is it, and your hair *is* a part of you.' The firmness and aptness of this comment are genuinely surprising to Mr Hewitt – this is in truth a two-way dialogue. The extract seems to us evidence of how, with patience and skill, pupils, however reluctant, can be encouraged to think cogently on matters of personal concern in a dialogue which is satisfying to both teacher and child.

It sometimes seemed though that the language available to the Hillview children had serious limitations in adequately conveying the complexity even of their first-hand experience. Miss Jones had comparatively little difficulty in establishing a friendly relationship with Richard and Len and they talked freely with her. But fluency in itself is not necessarily an indication of linguistic competence. The following conversation was carried on at a fair pace:

LEN (*of Richard's brother*): When was it he got done over?

RICHARD: Yeah that was he.

LEN: With his girlfriend. It was over in a lane wasn't it?

RICHARD: Yeah, his girlfriend got assaulted by four blokes, and he got done over.

MISS JONES: What do you mean, beaten up?

RICHARD: Yeah.

LEN: Smashed up, you know.

MISS JONES: Why?

RICHARD: Someone dropped the boot on him, another hit him in the stomach and one pushed him against the brick wall.

MISS JONES: Why was that?

RICHARD: I dunno.

LEN: Felt like it.

MISS JONES: Perhaps he was protecting his girlfriend?

LEN: He couldn't.

MISS JONES: Did they have some sort of disagreement? Was it something to do with gangs?

RICHARD: He didn't even see them before – he's never seen them before.

LEN: They was walking along and all of a sudden they just come along in a car, just stopped, just jumped out and clobbered them.

RICHARD: Out of the van.

MISS JONES: Were they drunk?

RICHARD: No.

MISS JONES: Was it the night?

RICHARD: Was it night – yeah – well if you've been down town you just do's that for a laugh.

MISS JONES: Some laugh! It's not a laugh is it?

RICHARD: It is.

MISS JONES: Do you think so?

RICHARD: Yeah.

MISS JONES: How is it funny then?

RICHARD: Well we do's that down our way.

MISS JONES: Well if you say something is a laugh then presumably it's funny – it tickles you.

LEN: It's a joke.

RICHARD: Yeah.

MISS JONES: A joke. Well if you were beaten up I don't think you'd consider it funny, would you?

RICHARD: I was done over the other night by a nineteen-year-old kid.

LEN: Yeah, he just comes up to him, drops the boot on him. I was in the pictures.

MISS JONES: That's a laugh is it?

RICHARD: Yeah.

MISS JONES: To you – you think it's a laugh.

RICHARD: I think it's a laugh, yeah – now it's all over, yeah.

MISS JONES: I bet you were scared.

RICHARD: I didn't even know nothing of it – he just comes up – smashed me on the back of my neck – when I turned round he hit I in the eye and I got all my gum cut in the inside ... I think that's funny.

One of the functions of talk is to represent to ourselves and others past experiences, sorting out the elements which make up their complexity, and through the selection and shaping of the telling to take up a considered attitude towards them. It is a way of reducing the confusion of the immediate to some sort of order. The difficulty is to do this without losing the subtleties of the sensations, feelings and complex attitudes of the original experience. It is perhaps only when experience is considered in all its fullness that we can learn from it and use it to meet new experiences with greater certainty. In a sense it could be said that Richard has managed to shape the violent events he describes. But he seems to use the verbal tag 'it's a laugh' as a convenient slot in which to place the beatings-up that he describes. Its inadequacy is evident: it reduces what must have been a confused and terrifying experience to a meaningless cliché. He is able to describe a series of events, but conveys nothing of his own feelings, and seems to regard violence as an inevitable and not-to-be-questioned occurrence. The language he uses about it no doubt reflects the cultural pattern of these boys of Hillview, who for reasons of bravado perhaps need to assert their masculinity before Miss Jones and one another.

The point remains that she is quite unable to get them to see the incongruity of the word 'funny' in this context. Several times she questions their use of the term, but in each case the boys evade the issue:

MISS JONES: How is it funny then?
RICHARD: Well we do's that down our way ...
MISS JONES: ... Well if you were beaten up I don't think you'd consider it funny, would you?
RICHARD: I was done over the other night by a nineteen-year-old kid.

A little later Richard seems almost ready to venture on a more detached view of what had happened: 'I think it's a laugh ... now it's over'. Miss Jones tries to get him to acknowledge his feelings about the incident, but he will have none of this and instead provides further gory details. He ends by reiterating his view that the incident was funny. There is a formidable problem here. Both the subcultural values of the boys and the patterns of the language available to them make it difficult for them, first to represent their experience adequately and then to detach themselves sufficiently from it to make valid generalizations.

Richard's narrative of the events, though vivid, lacks the specificity which would convey its uniqueness and at the same time enable the hearer to share in it imaginatively. The phrases 'drop the boot' and 'done over', though striking to us perhaps at first hearing because of their unfamiliarity, in fact reduce both the incidents to a flat sameness and make it difficult for us to understand exactly what happened. Part of Richard's problem is that to convey adequately the kind of situation that he was involved in would require more extended utterances than he seems capable of. A feature of his account is its short-windedness; he seems unable to sustain his narrative and proceeds with relatively short single statements describing what happened. Miss Jones tries by her questions to draw out some of the details – 'Perhaps he was protecting his girlfriend?' 'Were they drunk?' 'Was it the night?' but without success.

Still less is Richard able to relate the separate parts of the incident in any coherent way. For instance, Miss Jones tries to get
at the reasons for the beating-up of Richard's brother. *Why*
was he 'smashed up', she asks. Richard replies by simply giving
more details of the beating-up. Again she tries – 'Why was
that?' – at which Richard gives up altogether with the answer,
'I dunno.' Miss Jones was evidently a sympathetic and interested listener and gave Richard every opportunity to expand
on what was clearly a good story. Yet he cannot do so even
though these were as good conditions for talk as one could
expect. The only way he can learn to use language to explore
adequately the fullness of his experience is through further
opportunities of this kind. What is required though is first, the
sense that his experience might be of interest to others and,
second, the ability to shape it with the listener's needs in mind.
It is as though Richard assumed egocentrically that Miss Jones
was operating within the same context as himself and that
therefore a bare recital of facts would be sufficient. Paradoxi-
cally, his inability to take Miss Jones's view of things into
account is an aspect of the absence of any clear sense of the
importance of his own individuality. He experiences the whole
sequence of events as a member of a group rather than as an
individual – 'well if you've been down town you just do's that
for a laugh', 'Well we do's that down our way.' He seems to
think that his own feelings or anything that made the experience unique to himself as an individual can be of no relevance.

Essentially, what we are dealing with here are the Hillview
children's expectations about their place in the social structure,
expectations which have been built up from the beginning at
home and at school. Their low status and that of their peers and
families will have tended to create an environment in which
individual experience and self-awareness are undervalued.
There is an emphasis upon identification with the values of the
group and a reluctance to take up an individual stance for fear
of appearing different. These attitudes are in turn reinforced
by the nature of the language the Hillview children have at
their command. It does not give them the means to analyse

what happens to them nor the power to attain sufficient detachment to break free. In such a situation it is hardly surprising perhaps that physical violence plays so large a part in their lives. For them language has not been experienced as the instrument of power it is for those who can use a wider range of linguistic resources. The middle-class child grows up in a home where the adults expect to be able to get what they want through verbal negotiation. It is common for the family to use language to plan the use of time and money. There is an emphasis upon rational discussion, the child is rewarded for being able to give a verbal coherent account of himself and his actions. What he has to say is valued and the adults around him take an informed interest in the development of his linguistic skills. The child is encouraged continually to extend his use of talk and to operate its powerful resources. By contrast, many children like those of Hillview come from families living in overcrowded homes, with parents who, because of their working conditions or social assumptions, are unable to provide the continuity of interest the children need. What they say may be attended to only casually and sporadically; they may not be encouraged to elaborate on what they say in the interest of greater specificity or logic, and they may have comparatively little sense of language as an aid to understanding the past and planning the future. It is unlikely for them that language will be experienced as a source of satisfaction or a means to power. Not surprisingly, the middle-class child entering the 'verbal culture' of the secondary school has the advantage. He is used to consulting with adults, and has some familiarity with the advantages of the planned way of life implied by school rules and regulations and formal classroom procedures. He has the verbal means to take on whatever positions of responsibility the school has to offer in the way of form captain, school prefect or secretary of school societies. The working-class child loses out in all these respects.

The Hillview children's inability to 'work the system' of the secondary school, through their lack of acquaintance with the more elaborated forms of language, is only part of their problem. The kinds of difficulty we have been discussing – the failure to be specific about experience, the reluctance to articulate individual feeling or opinion, and a relative incapacity for making high-order abstractions – will all militate against learning. Much of the secondary-school curriculum is organized at a level of abstraction beyond the reach of these children's linguistic resources. The concepts and the language characteristics of subjects on the time-table often involve a level of generality which assumes considerable skill in the verbal organization of particular experiences. For all children, concepts such as 'democracy', 'climate' or 'energy' are only properly understood as the result of a developmental progression in thinking from the concrete to the abstract. The secondary school tends to assume that all children of a given chronological age are at a stage of development which makes it feasible to present material at a relatively abstract level. The child from a home with a rich and varied verbal culture is often able to hold his own among these abstractions from the moment he enters the secondary school: the child with limited linguistic resources will be handicapped from the beginning. Much of what the teacher says, the language of textbooks and the emphasis on learning through the written word, will all conspire to make the experience of school mystifying or incomprehensible.

Certainly the students on the Hillview project found the children's accounts of their experience in school very confused. There was very little evidence of enthusiasm for learning or any sense of engagement in their school work. When they did report to the students on what they were doing it was in a way which suggested that they had only a hazy notion of what was required of them:

MISS EMERY: Have you got any work that you ought to be doing tonight?

ELSIE: Only a bit, last night that was only two sums.

AMY: That was easy.

ELSIE: I had them wrong then. (*Giggles.*)

AMY: I told you I was right, didn't I?

ELSIE (*surprised*): Did you get them right?

AMY: Yeah.

ELSIE: So was mine right then.

AMY: It wasn't, 'cause you copied ...

ELSIE: Not the first one, I didn't copy the first one ... copied the second one though.

MISS EMERY: Did you have much homework last night?

AMY: She said we had to do these pur ... purchase things, said like twenty-two, she worked out you had to take away like two shillings from the twenty pounds – instead of you got to take, you got to times the two by twenty, that was forty, then take forty – then take two pounds away from the twenty, 'cause it was forty shillings, wasn't it?

ELSIE: Mmm ...

Amy's attempt to report what the teacher had asked them to do for homework reveals more than a merely verbal inadequacy. She seems not to have comprehended at all the thought processes involved. Her attempt to explain the procedures which the teacher has tried to introduce shows that she has not generalized any principle but is tied to the context of one particular sum. Moreover, neither she nor Elsie appear to question their lack of understanding. They seem not to know that they have not understood and so are in no position to ask for clarification. If this is the situation for many of the children who become early school-leavers it is not surprising that they leave having learnt so little. The more able child who can make sense of most of what the teacher says will realize when he has not understood and will be able to ask for further explanations. Most teachers will respond to this and will take the opportunity to engage their pupils in the fruitful exploration of ideas satisfying to both. For the child who cannot even begin to engage in this kind of discourse the teacher's words will be experienced simply as a demonstration of his power. Since they have no meaning for him, they will tend to confirm his view of the teacher as a figure of authority intent more on asserting his superiority than offering anything of value to him. In this situation the child's response is likely to be withdrawal either

into apathy or into open hostility. It is striking how many of
the accounts early leavers give of their life in school contain
elements of violence. It is impossible to distinguish fantasy
from fact, but accounts of teachers 'getting mad and shouting',
of punishments and of beatings are common. It certainly seems
that these children experience a great deal of frustration in
school, and their inability to engage with their teachers in
meaningful talk must be an important contributory factor.

Chapter 7
What is to be Done?

We have been considering in some detail areas which are likely to present difficulty for the young teacher in coming to terms with reluctant learners. We propose in this final chapter to draw out some of the implications of this account of the Hillview project for teachers and teacher trainers.

The first and most obvious point is that the project places student teachers in a close and continuous relationship with two or three children. They are inevitably brought up sharply against the different values and assumptions which the early school-leaver has about school and life in general. Because the relationship extends over the academic year it can develop fully, from what is for some an initial 'culture shock' to what in many cases becomes sympathetic and friendly involvement. The duration of the relationships and the informality of the situation enable students and children to engage with one another as individuals. The reality of these encounters involves a different kind of learning from courses in child development or the problems of the adolescent. Essential as these are, they inevitably place the student in the position of an onlooker who sees the children he is to teach as 'them' rather than as 'you' and 'I-that-was'. On the project some students, certainly, found themselves in situations where they felt free to play alongside the young adolescents in their charge. In discussion afterwards too they were enabled to feel the force of the connection between the children's behaviour and their own at a similar stage. (We sometimes find in discussions with students outside the Hillview project a curious reluctance to acknowledge the reality or relevance of their own adolescent experience.) It is partly the unstructured nature of the project which allows this strongly personal quality to develop. In the classroom, because of the large numbers involved and the need to organize and structure work, it is all too easy to depersonalize the children, to think of the class as a unit with a collective personality. The student on teaching practice plunged into the classroom from the beginning will tend to see the whole class, or groups within it, as either 'good' or 'bad', and will find it difficult to remember what he knows, that he is really dealing with individual children.

Since for the most part students on the project work with two or three children, decisions about what to do or where to go are shared in by the student and the children, a fact which inevitably gives rise to disagreements and struggles for leadership. In a sense the student is in the role of the parent and the children are his 'family'. We have found for example that rivalries and attempts by individual children to take over the 'parent' at the expense of the others are common. Sometimes a child will attempt to contract out of the relationship by sulking or refusing to cooperate because he cannot have the student to himself. The student can easily become part of these manipulations and may succumb to the temptation to ally himself to the 'good' child and to drive out the 'bad'. This is sometimes justified on the grounds that since no headway can be made with the erring child it is better 'to cut your losses and concentrate on the cooperative ones' – a rationalization which has exact parallels within the school situation. This is not a common occurrence on the project; in most cases for both students and children the relationship becomes a binding one. Sometimes children who regularly truanted from school nevertheless turned up for the Wednesday afternoon meetings with the students. On the other hand, the very strength of these attachments created problems. Some children became overdependent, making unreasonable demands to gain the student's attention, perhaps lingering on in their flats long after a meeting was supposed to end. When children begin to feel secure in the relationship they often enter a phase of testing out the strength of the student's commitment to them by behaving outrageously in public, or in other ways deliberately challenging his authority. The very duration of the relationship makes the ending of it difficult and at the end of the year students have to come to terms with parting from the children. This can be a painful business and students are often reluctant to face up to it. Even when in tutorial discussion we attempt to draw their attention to the fact that the end is near they tend to deny that there is any issue, sometimes asserting that they and the children will feel nothing. Alternatively, they may take refuge in unrealistic arrangements to exchange letters or to continue meeting.

The tutorials which are an essential part of the Hillview project are designed to give students the support necessary to learn from the problems created in their small groups, with all their related emotional undercurrents. They can talk about their feelings and those of the children and achieve some measure of understanding and detachment. This is the point where we as tutors can usefully relate their experiences in this special situation to teaching in general. In the large class group children will compete for the teacher's attention, will test his commitment to them, and will project upon him some of the feelings of love or frustration they experience in their own families. The young teacher may need particular help in acknowledging this situation, since he himself has only recently emerged from the painful ambivalences of his own adolescent dealings with his family.

While the primary aim of the Hillview project was to enable the students to get to know two or three early leavers, they engaged in a wide variety of activities, as has already become clear. For the most part these were sporadic and short-lived – enthusiasm and perseverance did not come easily to children with a long history of failure and discouragement. Many of them were only too glad that each Wednesday afternoon could be accepted as it came. Students often reported that children were reluctant to plan ahead or use the time in any way that recalled the structure of the school situation. When relationships could develop despite these feelings, student and children were sometimes able to arrive together at a project which extended over a number of weeks. The informality of the situation allowed them to discover just what they wanted to do, though the student had to take care to nurture the children's interest, neither hurrying them on too fast nor allowing the emotional tensions of the group to take over. It was not until the ninth week with her children that Miss Perkins, for instance, felt able to make a suggestion about a project they might do together. She was with her two girls at the local ice-skating rink.

Meeting 9. Both girls went off on the ice and left me at first, but when they saw me going round the rink with one of the other student's girls they came and grabbed me and the relationship seemed back on its feet again after that.

I suggested to them that they might make a movie film. Gwen didn't understand what I meant but Cathy explained. Cathy was definitely enthusiastic and asked if we could show it to their class afterwards. Gwen appeared uninterested as usual. The ideas they suggested were dreadful but the process of making a film and seeing themselves might be valuable.

Meeting 10. Started off by going into two junk clothes shops. I hoped that they might enjoy trying different clothes on and getting some ideas of what they could wear or how they could change themselves for the film. I suggested 'The Transformation of Gwen and Cathy' as a possible approach to the film. They wouldn't try any clothes on but they did look through some of them. I tried some things on hoping that they might lose some self-consciousness and join me – no luck.

I then took them into the drama studio to see an exhibition of theatrical design drawings. Cathy reacted to the drawings – although she didn't think that they were good drawings – but ideas started coming into her head as to how she could make some of the clothes very easily. This led to ideas about foreign costume and she continued making suggestions all afternoon. Gwen – negative reaction. At my flat we talked about ideas and I asked them to write some down – I intended to record them but I failed to get the tape recorder to work. So Cathy started to design a costume for herself and drew very carefully a head-dress based on the sun's rays and a long dress, while Gwen designed possible eye make-up after saying that she could not draw clothes. I suggested they finished their work off at home – Cathy keen, Gwen not interested, but Cathy carried both girls' drawings home. I suggested that they both try and get hold of some old clothes – they said they would. Suggestion for next week – practise using stage make-up on their own faces at the school. Cathy's face lit up at the idea. Gwen – usual vacant expression.

Meeting 11. I walked into the class teacher's room at 1.50 having arranged to meet the girls at 2 p.m. The teacher said that the girls had become worried that I would be late turning up.

We were sandwiched between a couple of classrooms in a changing room adjoining a needlework room. I asked who was going to make who up and of course it was Cathy who wanted to make Gwen up. Cathy had brought some of her own make-up because she didn't like the school's stage make-up – it's dirty. It was very successful. Cathy enjoyed making Gwen up – exaggerated eyes – highlights on the face emphasized, although I didn't go on about bone structure too much in case they thought they were having an art lesson. Gwen seemed to enjoy being made up although I think she was worried about getting even more spots on her face. Cathy photographed Gwen when she had finished, which Gwen seemed to like in a rather embarrassed way. When Cathy asked what we were going to do next week I made the mistake of suggesting we made some paper clothes or went out somewhere. She immediately changed from being light-hearted and chatty to being quiet and sulky. This was presumably because she wanted to be made up and photographed, so I started talking to Gwen about making Cathy up next week and we agreed that this is what would happen. Cathy remained sulky but I think that she was really pleased that she would get a turn.

Meeting 12. As Cathy and Gwen didn't like the little room we were in last week we worked on the stage. I was amazed to find that Cathy had been working at home making some Indian clothes and a lassoo. She had brought a bag full of old clothes to try on and pieces of net. We used make-up which I had taken to the school. Good atmosphere.

With some difficulty, because there were window cleaners about, I persuaded them to dress up and I took photos of them outside. Cathy was dressed and made up as an Indian lassooing Gwen. They were very embarrassed about being photographed but underneath they liked the idea.

Miss Perkins was patient enough to allow the interests of the girls to emerge gradually. She begins practically and imaginatively by visiting the junk shop hoping that the old clothes would provide the girls with ideas, but is not deterred that their shyness prevents them from making the most of the opportunity. Throughout, Miss Perkins is relaxed enough to accept that the girls may not fall in exactly with what she has in mind for them, but never loses sight of her ultimate purposes. After Cathy has made Gwen up she suggests that they should go on to make some paper clothes, but she is sensitive enough to see Cathy's disappointment and tactfully suggests to Gwen that it should be Cathy's turn to be made up next week. It is not that she is being distracted from her aims, but she is able to modify the means of getting there according to the particular needs of the children. It is here that one of the girls, Gwen, is peculiarly reluctant to display openly any kind of interest, yet Miss Perkins does not harass nor abandon her. She is not indifferent to Gwen's awkwardness – her comment about her spots perhaps suggests some aggressive feeling – but she is able to carry her along, unobstrusively helping her to take part in what they are doing. The unstructured nature of the Hillview project enabled some of the students to develop over time appropriate learning situations for these reluctant children. It may have helped them to a broader understanding of the nature of teaching and learning than more traditional classroom experience does. But of course the project was not designed specifically as a means of training students directly in class-teaching techniques. Any teacher-training programme must include, as well as this kind of 'unstructured' experience, opportunities for students to carry out structured work projects with small groups of children. It is here that they will learn to plan a sequence of work for particular groups of children in a situation sufficiently non-threatening to allow them to modify their plans as the occasion demands. Such projects would normally be related to subject work specifically designed to help students learn how to operate effectively in the classroom.

What the Hillview project may do, though, is to make students aware of the way in which they as potential teachers can engage with reluctant learners in cooperative activities. As mutual trust increases they may learn to recognize and help children who are discouraged to cope with the emotional factors which impede their learning. They may learn too to tolerate the frustration caused by what often appears as stubbornness or indifference, and be better able to approach the children with the generosity of spirit that is quite essential. The degree of professional resilience that is needed in dealing with reluctant learners cannot be overestimated. The teacher has to be able to accept rebuffs and backslidings and not be distracted from his intention to work with the children. As we have suggested throughout, this is very much a matter of understanding the reasons for the children's behaviour and the teacher's own responses to it. One of the aims of the project was to give the students some insight into the dynamics of the small-group situation they were working in. Through the exchange of anecdotes in the group tutorials they can be helped to see some of the patterns of behaviour which operate in any group and which often interfere with its overt task. The forces, largely unconscious, of hostility towards the leader of the group, rivalry for his attention, ganging-up to reject one member or stereotyping individuals into roles which they are compelled to maintain, may gradually emerge and be recognized for what they are. Once recognized they become less threatening, and less likely to overwhelm the student teacher and destroy his capacity to work with the group.

The apprehensions and the fantasies which arise in a small group operate at least as powerfully in the large group of the classroom. The teacher has equal need of insight into the dynamics of groups so that he can attain some measure of detachment. He has to be able to interpret the behaviour of the class, distinguishing between those aspects which arise from specific features of a particular lesson and those which originate in the currents of feeling common to any large group. For instance, it may be that he has failed to clarify a task he has set to the class, and the resulting disorder would be quite different in kind from the behaviour which arises when several members of the class compete for the attention of a new teacher. The teacher has responsibility for both kinds of situation, but in the case of the second he needs to be assured that these forces operate inevitably and are not a result of his ineffectiveness. They will occur in the classrooms of the most experienced teachers – an understanding of them may help him to ensure that they are used to promote rather than disrupt learning.

Our feeling is that the reluctant learner in the large teaching groups normal in our secondary schools is peculiarly vulnerable to the emotional climate of the classroom. Because the academically oriented tasks set by teachers are often less than immediately rewarding, his relationships with teachers and other members of the class are likely to be particularly important. Feelings about the teacher influence all children's capacity to learn, but for the less able this becomes critical. Equally, all children attach great importance to their relations with their peers, but for the reluctant learner these are of overriding significance. It is essential that there should be time and space in the secondary-school curriculum for these relationships to be fostered. This is not simply a matter of providing a registration period where a class-teacher can 'get to know the children', in the midst of collecting dinner money or filling in the register. Nor is it a matter of providing special counselling facilities, though these may be desirable. Essentially, it is necessary for every teacher to allow time in his planning of lessons for establishing and maintaining a good working relationship. He has to make himself open to the feelings of the class, allowing them opportunity to express their attitude to the work in hand and, by implication, to him. This is no easy matter: large classes, often consisting solely of 'failures', pressure on the teacher to fulfil the norms of the syllabus, and emphasis on administrative convenience rather than concern with individual needs, are all institutional features which may frustrate any teacher's best intentions. Within his own classroom however the teacher does have some autonomy, and can do much to create an emotional climate which acknowledges the force of children's relationship with one another. Given some understanding how, for less able children particularly, their feelings of friendship and hostility for their peers can so easily override the demands of academic work, the teacher can take deliberate steps to use this interest to further learning. In the first instance it is a matter of the teacher setting himself the task of making contact with each individual child, of informing himself of the web of relationships within the whole group, and taking an active interest in the way they fluctuate and develop. This is not a matter simply of observation or of administering sociograms or whatever, but of a personal engagement with the social life of the class. A few minutes at the beginning of a lesson, spent in a friendly exchange about the previous day's happenings or asking how a particular child is getting on, are not time wasted. And it is out of the relationships established in this way that the teacher can begin to break down a large class into smaller working groups, where the positive emotional climate set up can be mobilized for learning. Discouraged learners in particular can easily get into the habit of taking up a 'fighting' stance in relation to any teacher, because many of the approaches to learning they have experienced in the past have only emphasized their own inadequacy. Work in smaller groups does have the advantage that it discourages both children and teacher from operating stereotypes about one another, since it more easily allows individual differences to emerge. Of course, time is needed for the less able child to become engaged in structured learning. His relative immaturity, together with a long experience of failure, make the traditional organization of the timetable particularly inappropriate. The arbitrary division of the day into periods of a prearranged length is certain to bear little relation to the ebb and flow of his interest. It must be possible somewhere in the curriculum for an interest once aroused to be followed through as long as it can be sustained. There needs to be time too for periods of a kind of recuperation, when a child may savour the pleasure of having completed one task and begin to cast about for the next.

What is crucial is that teachers should establish a dialogue with reluctant learners which will enable them to reveal what they feel beyond the easy stereotyped responses and where their real interests lie. There are difficulties about this which we have already discussed. The language of school and the language of the children are very different: the teacher's way of talking may take for granted values and attitudes which are in fact quite alien to the child and, at the secondary level in particular, may operate at a level of generality which is not yet within his reach. Yet if they are to profit from what secondary education offers, then from the first year at school they must be engaged by teachers in a continuous and stimulating dialogue about the *particularities* of their experience. Most children, of whatever class or level of ability, arrive at the age of eleven with a lively curiosity, ready to trust the teacher and delighted to talk about anything and everything. It is especially important for the less able children that these qualities are fostered by the teacher, not suppressed in the interest of a premature insistence on formal learning. They need ample opportunities to talk about themselves and their experience, and to relate this experience to the purposes of the teacher. He may, for instance, offer concrete examples in a particular subject area, allow children to present what seem to them relevant examples of their own, and then help them to discover some kind of generalization appropriate to their stage of development. This is a slow process – the teacher must feel free to attend to all that the children offer, however irrelevant it may seem. Sometimes their contributions will show him what they have not understood rather than what they have, and where they are less relevant, he has to try to discern the mental processes involved, looking for common ground which will aid the learning he has in mind. He has to resist the temptation simply to reject what seems beside the point or to hurry on to the next stage demanded by the syllabus. The teacher himself is under pressure from such demands and from the expectation of the school that certain ground will be covered in the time allotted.

A further difficulty is that, although ready to talk about events, the children we have been discussing are less familiar with the use of language to define personal feelings and opinions. Even the teacher convinced of the need will have difficulty in persuading these children that their individual experience is of value. It may take time for him to establish the kind of supporting relationship which will make the child confident of this. Unfortunately, time and the conditions which make personal interchange possible are commodities in short supply in too many of our schools. Certainly the kind of dialogue we have in mind is almost impossible if the teacher addresses himself solely to the class as a whole. We have already suggested that teachers who recognize this can go some way towards solving the problem by arranging smaller working groups within the classroom. Even so they will find it very difficult to give sufficient attention to each of the groups. Much may be achieved by planning the work so that the children are required to talk to one another. In such semi-formal situations they can begin to acquire confidence in their own powers of self-expression and in their ability to engage in constructive dialogue. However, when the whole class consists of children with restricted language ability the likely result will simply be a reinforcement of existing skills and attitudes. It is vital that, for some of the time at least, children, like those from Hillview should work alongside others with more highly developed linguistic resources. The teacher then can take steps to supplement the help *he* gives, by virtue of being an adult speaker, with the informal exchanges among the children which will arise when they are engaged on a joint task. Rigorous streaming can only isolate the less able child from the range of linguistic experience the school could offer. Where the proper context of talk is established in this way there is at least a chance that the less able child will learn to acquire the more abstract ways of thinking necessary for his educational development. The skills of writing, too, with the opportunities they offer for the reflective handling of experience, may have a chance to flourish when a more confident participation in the oral culture of the school has been established.

The situation is urgent. Even with an extra year available children like those from Hillview cannot be educated unless all teachers understand the role of language in social and intellectual development. More specifically, they need to know

how central talk is to learning, and they must be practised
in the strategies that will enable them to use what children say
to help their advance to more complex modes of thought and
feeling. Whatever experience children bring to school, whatever language they are able to express it in, must be valued as
the only possible starting-point for their educational development.

The fact of the matter is that as schools are at present the
experience and contribution of these reluctant learners are
not valued. The school, whatever its declared policy, largely
operates to reinforce the low status that these children have in
society at large. Our secondary schools are seen by themselves
and others primarily as institutions devoted to the achievement
of success defined in extremely limited terms. Learning is
identified with a competitive scrambling for marks and examination successes, the fruits of office are a reward for social
conformity, and responsibility is regarded as a privilege to be
awarded to the few. What the school offers in the way of
teaching children to think, to understand themselves and
others and the environment they live in, is made conditional
upon their acceptance of a whole range of social norms which
have little to do with education, but are an aspect of the lower-
middle-class ethos of the school. Obsessional insistence on
punctuality, compulsory attendance at mass prayer, niggling
attention to uniformity of dress – all represent pressures on the
child to conform. They add up to a kind of depersonalization,
a denial of children's individuality in the attempt to force all
into a common mould which is believed to simplify the school's
task. The very vehemence with which these social norms are insisted upon indicates that there is more than organizational
convenience at stake. The root of the insistence on orderliness
at all costs lies surely in an irrational fear of adolescence itself.
Some teachers' preoccupation with length of hair or skirt, with
width of trouserleg or colour of stockings, indicates the sexual
tension and envy which underlie a good deal of the adult's attitude to the adolescent. When there is added to this general fear
of adolescents, the middle-class teacher's apprehension about

the working-class child's standards of behaviour we have a potentially explosive situation. Fear gives rise to repression, repression leads to hostility, hostility justifies fear – the vicious circle is established. Middle-class and able children can deal with the intricacies of the system of control operated by the school and can get from it what they need. The less able working-class child is in a very different position: many of the niceties of behaviour demanded by the school will seem meaningless yet will take up a disproportionate amount of his time and energy to negotiate. Failure to live up to the school's expectations about his appearance or his demeanour in the classroom will arouse the disapproval of his teachers, and this may easily lead him to reject them and all they stand for. Effectively access to learning is denied to them on grounds of social class. It is essential that these children be accepted into schools unconditionally. Their academic progress should not involve them in a denial of their individuality, nor do violence to the culture that has sustained them up to that point. We do not underestimate the difficulties involved in all this. For one thing, the children themselves will not easily accept that the teacher's motives are disinterested. Hard experience may have taught them to take pride in their reputation for intractability. Friendly overtures may be rejected or exploited, and it takes considerable resilience and persistence on the part of a teacher to establish a genuinely accepting relationship with them. When the children arouse feelings of anger and frustration in him, as they certainly will, there will be a strong temptation to respond in a punitive way – too strong to be resisted sometimes, but it is essential that he avoids an escalation of conflict. A considerable degree of detachment and self-understanding is needed at this point and a level of maturity which the children by definition cannot possess. It may be that the teacher and the school as a whole have to learn to tolerate behaviour which has in the past seemed inappropriate. Many successful teachers of less able working-class children find it possible to accept that children address them and one another with easy familiarity in the classroom, and can take in their stride such things as personal comments on dress and appearance. There seems little doubt that a genuine acceptance of the working-class child in the secondary school will involve schools in some quite radical readjustments. Manners will be freer, there will be tolerance of a greater spontaneity in children's responses to what happens, relations between children and teachers will be less reserved. Motivation based upon an appeal to the individual's desire to better himself will give way to an emphasis on the satisfactions of working with others for a common goal. The rewards the school offers will be based not upon desert but upon need. The resources of the school, however limited, will be made available to these less able children quite as much as to the more successful.

More than this is needed though: if their status is to be raised then they must be included in whatever process the school has for consulting pupils about what it does. If there is a prefect system, for example, or some better form of sharing out responsibility for running the school, then these children must be called upon to play their part too. (This will mean, for instance, that prefects will be drawn from fourth and fifth years rather than from the sixth form alone.) Where there is a school council it should again be a deliberate policy to incorporate the less able working-class child. It has to be deliberate because such children will not necessarily emerge as the 'natural' leaders – their need is to be given the opportunity to *learn* to take responsibility, and this can be done only by exercising it, not at all by exhortation.

Comprehensive schools offer opportunities for all this to happen – in theory at least, children of all levels of ability and from different social classes are catered for within the same institution. However, partly because they are under pressure at present to compete with selective schools, their organization and methods of teaching can make them no less socially divisive than schools have been in the past. In any case, the divisiveness endemic in society at large cannot be simply eradicated by the school alone. An understanding of the school as an institution may nevertheless provide teachers with the basis for making those changes that are within their scope. The less able working-class child, for instance, would have a better chance in the secondary school if there were less emphasis upon the inhibiting rituals that serve to control life within it. A great deal of the energy and ingenuity of head and staff is still devoted to measures designed to induce a kind of unthinking tribal loyalty. In the school's external relations this manifests itself in the form of a suspicious, even hostile stance towards outsiders – parents, inspectors, and other visitors. Internally there is an emphasis on conformity and upon bringing credit to school or house through success in examinations and games. When children cannot identify with these tribal aspirations they fall away into a state of apathy or open hostility. To meet the needs of the less successful working-class child schools must be 'detribalized'. Anxieties aroused by exhortation to meet collective and often inappropriate standards of behaviour and achievement can be reduced if there is emphasis rather upon relating the goals set to the particular needs of the individual. The school must become a more open community, where children can be themselves and sufficiently at ease to accept the learning opportunities the teachers offer them. They should be able to work at the pace and in the style appropriate to their stage of development, and to feel sufficiently valued as persons to work easily alongside their more able fellows. A reduction in competition as an incentive, with the substitution of the satisfaction derived from tasks completed in ways appropriate to the individual learner, will help the school to become an 'accepting' community which welcomes individual and social differences.

The developments advocated here to improve the lot of the reluctant learner cannot be brought about by teachers working in isolation. The individual teacher who is trying to go it alone, though he may have a limited success, will eventually be driven into a state of exhausted despair. Change can only come when the habit of consultation is established as a normal procedure in the making and carrying out of policy within the school. The individual teacher must feel free to consult with colleagues or the head over problems or new approaches, without feeling either that his competence is in question or that he is usurping the authority that properly belongs to others. Staff meetings must be genuinely consultative, with the power to make decisions affecting large issues of policy, rather than simply providing a platform for the head or the occasion for lengthy discussion of administrative detail. The role of the head is crucial in all this. He is in a peculiarly isolated position, often required to act as a ceremonial figurehead of authority yet resented for carrying out the very function for which is he appointed. Teachers use him as a punitive figure to apply simplistic solutions to problems which can only be properly dealt with by consultative means. He is himself subject to pressures from outside the school, from governors, local councillors, the education authority and parents, which may have the effect of reducing his capacity to act independently. He has somehow to reconcile the conflicting demands made upon him, quite different in kind from what he may have experienced as an assistant teacher. It is one of the curiosities of our educational system that people are appointed to this most crucial position without any training in the managerial and other skills required. The effect is that the existing structure of the school tends to be perpetuated, since the only model newly appointed heads can draw upon derives from their 'internal apprenticeship' in other schools. And since this experience has served them well they may find it difficult to conceptualize and carry through a radically different pattern. Part of the problem is that neither they nor their staff are likely to have experienced working in a fully consultative way.

A school which has established means of consultation at all levels and which can tolerate diversity is able to incorporate new members comfortably, whether they be student teachers or probationers. The young teacher is in a very vulnerable position, anxious about his competence and uncertain of his status. His very anxiety often reduces his capacity to assimilate necessary information about the school, disposition of rooms, routine registration procedures, use of school facilities and so on. It is seldom enough simply to outline all this in the first two or three days of term. Even more difficult to convey quickly are the unspoken rules and taboos of the institution. Many a young teacher has unwittingly offended by sitting in a chair sacred to some senior member of staff or by failing to show due deference to a head prefect. There need to be some established procedures for familiarizing the young teacher with the ways of the school. It may be that an experienced member of staff should be appointed to see the newcomer through the first year, with regular meetings at which issues can be frankly raised and discussed. Perhaps the most pressing need is for a lighter teaching timetable, so that this introductory process can be realistically carried through.

Our chief concern in this book is with the problems of the young teacher in relation to the reluctant learner, and what is difficult enough for any teacher joining the profession becomes even more demanding when he is faced with their peculiar needs. It is not unknown for young teachers to be given the most difficult classes from the very beginning, a procedure which undoubtedly has driven many from the profession altogether. A considerable proportion of young teachers want to take on work with less able children, but it is important that their introduction to such work should be a gradual one, with more experienced members of staff providing support and professional guidance. It may be that this whole situation will be eased as more schools give up the rigid streaming of children according to their ability and as staff collaborate more in team-teaching approaches. Where this is the case and where frequent consultation is the rule it becomes much easier to incorporate a new member, encouraging him where he is uncertain and making use of and openly acknowledging the skills and resources he will certainly have.

The student teacher on school practice is in a very similar situation to the young teacher in his first job. He too has to some extent to be incorporated into the community of the school and to be supported while he begins to learn his trade. The difference is that he is in the school for a relatively short

time and that the responsibility for his learning is shared between the school and the teacher-training institution. He has
relatively low status and is in the position of having to serve
two masters – a situation which easily gives rise to fantasy and
manipulation. Too often student, teacher and teacher trainer
are unclear about their respective functions and work in an
uneasy state of mutual deception. The situation can only be
resolved if there is genuine collaboration between all three
parties. The student must be able to acknowledge that while on
school practice he is a learner, and that there is no expectation
that he should operate from the beginning as a 'real' teacher.
His need to prove his competence must not lead him to deny the
difficulties that inevitably arise, nor to feel unable to discuss
them frankly with both teacher and supervising tutor. The
teacher in the school, with responsibility for students, must
feel that his part in the process is recognized as being essential.
Help with the training of students should be seen as a natural
extension of the competent teacher's role, as a way of making
more widely available his expertise in particular subject areas
or with particular groups of children. This means that he must
be centrally involved in the teacher-training programme, working side by side with the teacher trainer. Only when the teacher
works in this way with the college or university tutors can he
really know precisely what his particular function is. Clearly
this collaborative approach makes further demands on the time
of busy teachers and requires that it be taken into account
when the school timetable is made up and allowances are
distributed. The head who values the stimulus that work of this
kind can provide for his staff will release them for meetings at
college or university department, and make time available for
them to work with students within the school. This need not be
seen as a one-sided bargain: there is no reason why schools
should not plan their work in the knowledge that there will be
students available at different times through the year. Although
they will not be experienced teachers – and should not be used
as such – they can be involved with the school staff on schemes
of work which demand more manpower than is usually avail-

able. The students certainly have skills and talents which can be drawn upon from the beginning, and we have already given ample evidence showing how much children, particularly the less able, benefit from closer contact with adults.

The stress we have placed on the more positive role that teachers can play in the training of students should not be taken to imply that we think the more practical part of the work can be done by the school alone. The supervisor from college or department of education has a vital part to play in the process. Although committed to preparing students to function effectively in the classroom, precisely because he is not a member of the school staff he has the detachment necessary to help the student to see beyond the immediate stress of the teaching practice. Through discussion he can help him to interpret what is happening, relate it to his reading, and begin to make valid generalizations of his own about children and teaching. It is important too that the student should be able to get advice from more than one source. He may be better able to do this in a realistic way if he knows that teacher and supervisor work together in a relationship less defensive than is sometimes the case at present. There may be opportunities for students, teachers and supervising tutors to plan work jointly, and this would help above all else to dispel the common illusion that theory and practice are two quite separate entities.

Finally, if the greater degree of consultation that we have recommended is to become a reality, teachers themselves must, as part of their own training, become used to this way of working. Teacher-training institutions must be organized in such a way that the processes and procedures of consultation are learnt by students as an integral part of the training. Those of us engaged in teacher training, ourselves often the products of hierarchically organized grammar schools, may have difficulty in adapting ourselves to these new organizational patterns. There is strong pressure on us to prove the respectability of what we do by clinging to procedures which owe more to a faded academicism than to the new demands that schools make upon teachers. If the courses we offer are to prepare students to teach children of all abilities and from all social backgrounds they must include accounts of relevant research into the nature of learning, the structure of institutions and differences of social class. At the same time students must be enabled to relate what they read or hear about these areas of knowledge to what they see done or do themselves. We must acknowledge that the analysis of actual experience and planning for future action are quite as intellectually demanding as any more traditionally based academic study. Moreover, student teachers will themselves be more likely to collaborate with their colleagues in schools, if they see that their tutors and lecturers in colleges and departments of education habitually work in this way. The curriculum of most teacher-training institutions in fact is quite as fragmented as that of any school.

As we have suggested, all children will suffer from any inadequacies in the preparation of teachers but of all children the less able working-class child suffers most. He too is the child who does most to make the life of ill-prepared young teachers intolerable. We recognize only too clearly that some of the changes in our schools that are essential to give these children any chance of a decent education do not depend upon the schools alone. Society itself must change. In the meantime something can be done. In schools where staff have become accustomed to talking and working together, the young teacher is more likely to receive the encouragement and the information he needs to survive his early encounters with reluctant learners without losing his initial idealism. He may also feel sufficiently supported to collaborate with other teachers to question and to begin to change the institutional structure of the school, where it operates so clearly to the disadvantage of less able and less confident children. Only in this way can schools become places where the young teacher and the reluctant learner can co-exist in a properly educative relationship.

Further Reading

Barnes, D., Britton, J., and Rosen, H., *Language, the Learner and the School*, Penguin, 1969, rev. edn 1971.

Bernstein, B., 'Language and social class', *British Journal of Sociology*, November 1960.

Bernstein, B., 'Linguistic codes, hesitation phenomena and intelligence', *Language and Speech*, January–March 1962.

Bernstein, B., 'A socio-linguistic approach to social learning', in J. Gould (ed.), *Penguin Social Sciences Survey*, Penguin, 1965.

Bernstein, B., 'A critique of the concept of "compensatory education"', in D. Rubinstein and C. Stoneman (eds), *Education for Democracy*, Penguin, 1970.

Britton, J., *Language and Learning*, Allen Lane The Penguin Press, 1970.

Douglas, J. W. B., *The Home and the School*, MacGibbon & Kee, 1964.

Douglas, J. W. B., *All Our Future*, Peter Davies, 1968.

Ford, J., *Social Class and the Comprehensive School*, Routledge & Kegan Paul, 1969.

Fuchs, E., *Teachers Talk*, Anchor Books, 1969.

Goffman, E., *Asylums*, Anchor Books, 1961; Penguin, 1968.

Goffman, E., *Interaction Ritual*, Anchor Books, 1967.

Hargreaves, D. H., *Social Relations in the Secondary School*, Routledge & Kegan Paul, 1967.

Hines, B., *A Kestrel for a Knave*, Penguin, 1969.

Holt, J., *How Children Fail*, Pitman, 1964; Penguin, 1969.

Holt, J., *The Underachieving School*, Pitman, 1970.

Jackson, B., and Marsden, D., *Education and the Working Class*, Routledge & Kegan Paul, 1962; Penguin, 1966.

Jackson, P. W., *Life in Classrooms*, Holt, Rinehart & Winston, 1968.

Klein, J., *Samples from English Cultures*, vols. 1 and 2, Routledge & Kegan Paul, 1965.

Lawton, D., *Social Class, Language and Education*, Routledge & Kegan Paul, 1968.

Maizels, J., *Adolescent Needs and the Transition from School to Work*, Athlone Press, 1970.

Menzies, I. E. P., *The Functioning of Social Systems as a Defence against Anxiety*, Tavistock, 1961.

Rice, A. K., *Learning for Leadership*, Tavistock, 1965.

Richardson, E., *The Environment of Learning*, Nelson, 1967.

Rogers, C. R., *Client-Centred Therapy: Its Current Practice, Implications and Theory*, Houghton Mifflin, 1951.

School of Barbiana, *Letter to a Teacher*, Penguin, 1970.

Schools Council, *Young School Leavers*, HMSO, 1968.

Seabrook, J., *The Unprivileged*, Longman, 1967.

Strodtbeck, F. L., 'The hidden curriculum of the middle-class home', in A. H. Passow, N. M. Goldberg and A. J. Tannenbaum, *Education of the Disadvantaged*, Holt, Rinehart & Winston, 1967.

Wilmott, P., *Adolescent Boys in East London*, Routledge & Kegan Paul, 1966; Penguin, 1969.

Wolff, S., *Children under Stress*, Allen Lane The Penguin Press, 1969.

Yablonsky, L., *The Violent Gang*, Macmillan Co., 1962; Penguin, 1967.